Bank Role

SANDY McCARDLE

authorHOUSE®

AuthorHouse™ UK
1663 Liberty Drive
Bloomington, IN 47403 USA
www.authorhouse.co.uk
Phone: 0800.197.4150

Published by AuthorHouse 01/16/2017

ISBN: 978-1-5049-9512-2 (sc)
ISBN: 978-1-5049-9513-9 (hc)
ISBN: 978-1-5049-9514-6 (e)

CONTENTS

ACKNOWLEDGEMENTS

Without the help and encouragement of some friends and my two daughters Alexandra and Skye, this book would have been written.

With their help, writing this book was much easier. The author would especially like to thank the proprietors of Tatler magazine for their permission to reproduce the illustrated feature of The Queen Charlotte's Ball 1952.

My thanks to Daily Express/N&S Syndication for permission to reproduce newspaper article.

PREFACE

Charles Sinclair, my maternal grandfather, was a part owner of G&J McLachlan Ltd a Scottish whiskey distillery. His wife, my grandmother, Liz Jardine, talking about the future, would often end by saying "if we are spared." No doubt she obtained that expression from her knowledge of the bible derived during her strict Victorian Scottish Presbyterian upbringing.

In the arithmetic of life, alas, I find I am nearer the end rather than the beginning. As such, there were times when I wondered if "I would be spared" to finish this book the burden of ageing has few benefits. I have reached the inevitable stage where I can count my remaining friends on one hand, and have even entertained morbid thoughts on who of my remaining friends will be next to leave God's waiting room.

My father taught me "self praise is no honour." As a result of that teaching, like so many of us, I have had difficulty in taking credit for even quite modest achievements. Perhaps W S Gilbert's brilliant lyrics in the comic opera "Ruddygore" might be better advice for the ambitious. Quote "My boy you may take it from me, that of all the afflictions accursed with which a man's saddled and hampered and addled a diffident nature's the worst."

Chorus:

If you wish in the world to advance,
your merits your bound to enhance.
you must stir it and slump it, and blow your own trumpet,
or, trust me, you haven't a chance!"

As a child, following my christening in 1931, I regularly attended Sunday school. Since then I have been an intermittent church goer. I was married in church and my children were christened in church, and I have had the privilege to visit the Vatican and the holy places in Jerusalem. Against that background, I decided to think very deeply about faith. Here is the result.

FAITH

I believe in Christianity. However, I sometimes have difficulty in believing in God.

For me, Christianity is a man conceived religion that offers a way of conducting ones life governed by the Ten Commandments.

I have no difficulty in coming to terms with Christianity. I am a true believer in the Christian faith. I do, however, have difficulty in accepting some of the teachings of the bible. For example the virgin birth, and the resurrection. It seems to me that, over the years, much of the bible teachings have been embroidered to the point of incredulity.

For me, God, if there is one, is a focus of my religious beliefs. A sort of weak token faith. I do not believe he sits somewhere up there in judgement. I do not believe in life after death. Surely we all deserve to die without having to endure some sort of perpetual morphing? Death to me means death, the end of life. Having said that, if one has children, then, of course, one 's genes do live on. In that sense there IS life after death, for the progenitors.

Very often fair weather Christians coast along with doubts about the existence of God. It often takes an event of extreme peril or other adversity for them to instinctively offer a prayer to the almighty. Enacting this simple act of faith is an admission that, in their mind, there IS God, so it seems having faith, after all, is the simple answer to the age old question, does God exist? Put another way, doubters might ask, "Prove God exists!" To whom believers might reply "Prove he doesn't exist!"

I must say, I never thought I would ever write about religion. The ways of the Lord are strange indeed!

Shakespeare wrote about all the world being a stage and all the men and women players in it.

He went on to say that some men have many parts to play. In writing my memoirs I was surprised at the many roles I have played in life, the dominant one being that of a banker. This book is by no means in the nature of a banking treatise, it is more of a social commentary from the perspective of my various roles in life.

CHAPTER ONE

Early Days

1948, found me enjoying my first car. My Father gave me a Morgan 4/4 as a reward for passing my driving test - second attempt. I find the ownership of various cars at different times punctuates ones life to some extent. In writing about cars I am not so much interested in the cars per se, but rather my life at the time of using the vehicles.

David Heneage was often with me in the Morgan. He and I were in the same dormitory at Hartree School. Hartree was a minor Scottish boarding school for boys. Geoffrey Hardcastle was the head of the school and had a nick name for most of the pupils.

Heneage, who was the heir to Killochan Castle, was known as "that ersatz aristocrat".

Matthew McMillan, who enjoyed riding, was known as "that jockey thing". The son of the Lord Provost of Glasgow was overweight and, of course, was known as "tubby" Warren. I was not aware that I had a nickname but I do remember in class being compared to "Tim the Ostler with hair like mouldy hay." Geoffrey Hardcastle was a remarkable head master. Unusually for his time, he would include lessons on the appreciation of art and porcelain in our curriculum. On leaving school, I opted to do my national service early, and did not attend university until much later, when I obtained a diploma in business studies at the university of Hawaii.

On school holidays my father was keen that I should take school holiday jobs for work experience. I could never reconcile his expression "holiday job". It didn't make sense to me to be on holiday and yet have a job! The first job he found for me was for two weeks in a carpet factory. I had to clock in at 8am and work until 4pm with an hour off for lunch in the factory canteen. I was paid £3 for a five day week. My duties during the first week were to assist with the cleaning of skeins of wool yarn.

The yarn was placed on poles. These were then immersed in a series of hot water filled vats in order to clean off grease and dirt. The scoured yarn was then dyed ready for weaving. My second week was spent in the factory laboratory testing dyes and the breaking strength of random yarn samples. The carpet industry was booming in the immediate post WW2 years. I recall large quantities of carpet being sent to fit out new built ships in Clydebank, and a constant high volume of sales to carpet wholesalers.

During school holidays I was also allowed to work in my father's cinema. I helped to clean the toilets and collect litter after each show. The amount of litter was staggering, and consisted mostly of sweet papers and cigarette butts. I found the worst job was removing discarded chewing gum. Before each show I had the task of going round the seating with a large perfumed disinfectant spray. The projection room had Gaumont British equipment having carbon rods to produce the required intense projection light. There were two projectors working in tandem to ensure seamless transfers between reels. I was taught how to rapidly splice 35mm cinematography film. This skill was very necessary, and taught to everyone in case there was a break in the film during a show. On these occasions, the audience was quite unforgiving, and would stamp their feet until the screen picture was restored. My reward for working in the cinema was to be allowed occasionally to accompany my father on his visits to London on cinema business. We would attend trade shows, restricted to exhibitors, of newly released films very often at the Odeon in Leicester Square. The trade shows would usually begin at 11am and finish just in time for a late lunch over which we would discuss the merits of the films. After lunch we would make our way to Wardour Street, Soho and make the bookings with the distributors for Paramount, MGM, United Artists, RKO, Warner Bros, and others. Before release, a new film would go through three viewing stages. Firstly to obtain a category certificate, secondly the critics, and thirdly the exhibitors.

Most popular at the time were the gangster and cowboy films. The cowboy stars at that time were, Roy Rogers, Gene Autrey, Hopalong Cassidy. There was a joke about a nun called Hop Along Chastity. Popular gangster actors were George Raft, James Gagney and Edward G Robinson. I vividly remember lustfully appreciating Betty Grable's legs well displayed in her musicals. Distributing the numbered canisters of film to exhibitors was a complex business. Distribution was mainly by road or to the nearest railway station. It was up to the exhibitor to collect from and return film to the station or road depot on time. Box office profit was fairly predictable. This was augmented by profit from the sale of ice cream, sweets, and cigarettes. Before mass tv the cinema was the dominant medium in showbiz. With the advent of mass tv it gradually became a sunset industry, before consolidating to what it is to-day. On joining HSBC I was interested to read, in a lending guidance manual, that cinematograph film should not be taken as collateral, as it had no intrinsic value.

Fortunately, my father sold the business just before the impact of mass tv. At the time, he mentioned my grandfather was a backer for the first cinema in Glasgow.

At the end of WW2 my Father secured the lease of Belleisle, a notable country house set in large well maintained grounds on the outskirts of Ayr. The grounds included a golf course, woodlands, a conservatory, deer park, and well tended gardens. Of particular interest, was a magnificent carved wooden chimney piece in the entrance hall of the house. The carving depicts scenes from some of Robert Burn's works. One of the conditions of the lease was the provision of hotel and catering facilities. As a family in residence, we thus enjoyed the benefits of a well maintained fully staffed country house, with the added advantage of income from the hotel and catering activities. As a teenager I enjoyed living at Belleisle hugely. For some reason I did not take up golf even though the golf course was literary on my doorstep. Belleisle was near the river Doon estuary. At a certain time of the year I would walk to the river and witness shoals of salmon being commercially netted by fishermen. The hapless salmon were easy pickings, as they would congregate in the estuary in large numbers, in readiness to migrate up stream to spawn.

As a school boy in Scotland during the war, I was once co-opted to pick potatoes. It was part of the war effort there being a shortage of manpower. Some German and Italian prisoners of war were allowed to work on farms, if they volunteered. They were even allowed to keep their small earnings. For a back breaking 8 hour day I think I was paid about 5 shillings. The farmer's wife would make a huge cauldron of mashed potatoes for lunch, all of which would be devoured ravenously by the school boys and POW alike. We were not encouraged to fraternise with the prisoners. Also as a war time school boy I played my part in the downfall of Hitler by participating in door knock collections of aluminium pots and pans. These were melted down and made into aircraft parts for the RAF.

Infant. With Mama and sister Elizabeth 1932.

Schoolboy. Wartime Scotland

Teenager. First and last motorbike

In due course my Father gave up Belleisle whilst I was away with HSBC on a 4 year tour of Japan. It was not until I took up residence at Wardour Castle years later, that I would, once again, enjoy country living.

On a half term school holiday David Heneage invited me to stay at Killochan Castle. We took the train from Ayr to Girvan. When we alighted at Girvan station we were amazed to be confronted by David's stepfather, Captain Hodgekinson, on the platform, in handcuffs, attached to a policeman. He had been arrested for firing a shotgun at the ceiling in the castle drawing room knowing his wife was in the room above. It transpired he and his wife had an alcohol fuelled blistering row, culminating in the firearm offence. I never saw Captain Hodgekinson again. He and David's mama divorced not long after the shooting incident. At the firearm offence hearing, I believe he was let off with a caution. I spent many weekends at Killochan, mostly shooting and enjoying excursions to nearby Turnberry Hotel for afternoon tea. Nowadays Turnberry Hotel is owned by Donald Trump.

CHAPTER TWO

National Service

One of the highlights of my national service was dashing around Libya in a Humber armoured scout car. Utterly useless against road side bombs, and a variety of other missiles, but great fun to command.

On being called up for national service in 1949 I was selected for officer training by a War Office Selection Board, and thus became an officer cadet at Mons Officer Cadet School.

Once on early morning parade I fell foul of RSM Brittain, who was reputed to have the loudest voice in the British army. My friend Guy and I were on 6am early morning parade having just made it back to barracks after a night out in London.

RSM Brittain, pace stick in hand, and accompanied by a posse of drill sergeants was inspecting the ranks and stopped in front of me and my friend. He said to my friend, "Your boots are dusty, Sir". For some unaccountable reason the whole scenario struck me as very funny and I burst out laughing. RSM Brittain, apoplectic, stopped in his tracks, whirled round, and bellowed to his minions "Get that man off the square". I was immediately seized by two drill sergeants, and quick marched off the square into the guardroom. There I had time to reflect on how I could have possibly enraged a staff RSM instructor let alone RSM Brittain a renowned icon of the British Army. In the spartan, stark, secular atmosphere of the guardroom I took comfort in remembering an old Sunday school jingle "God likes to test those he loves the best."

I was eventually put on the bizarre charge of laughing on parade, and arraigned before the Commanding Officer. He was incredulous that anyone could laugh on parade. He asked me if I would laugh at an enemy attacking me with a bayonet? I had no answer for that, and was given the punishment of 4 extra guard duties to be carried out on alternate nights so as to avoid too much sleep deprivation.

My mother and father came to my passing out parade. My father generously paid for my uniforms. I managed to find a used Sam Browne belt, and a British Warm overcoat in Moss Bros. The rank insignia markings on the coat revealed the previous owner had been a captain. So with my one star I imagined people would think I had been demoted! It would be some time before I was gazetted from 2/Lt to Lieutenant.

I was posted to Tripoli and decided to treat myself to a room at the Savoy on my last night in London. I had a few drinks at Jules bar in Jermyn Street and in Shepherds market hoping to find some romance, but without success.

The next day I was on a troopship looking out to sea and feeling quite homesick.

On arrival at Tripoli we were all amazed to see camels trudging through snow caused by one of those freak Mediterranean cold snaps.

Mitchell Cotts handled our baggage and I opened a bank account with Banca di Roma by drawing a cheque on my Glyn Mills account.

The mess was a comfortable requisitioned Italian built villa with it's own beach and orange grove. As a young nineteen years old transport platoon commander, most of my of my time was spent on exercises going south as far as the Garian Caves in the Sahara, and west as far as Leptis Magna. I much enjoyed seeing the Roman remains at Leptis Magna.

In wartime, transporting troops and supplies to the front could be a hazardous occupation. There were stories of entire convoys being wiped out by enemy action such as, aircraft strafing, on and off shore bombardment, ambushes, shelling and tank fire, minefields and road side bombs. The cover of darkness was considered a Godsend, so much time was spent on night camouflaging exercises and convoy spacing.

Apart from one or two minor incidents requiring riot control, there was little trouble. Italian colonists were being repatriated and Colonel Gaddafi had not yet appeared on the scene.

Untouchable. Immunity from arrest by police in Egypt.

11

Peacekeeper. Anti riot patrol Libya 1950.

After about a year in Libya I embarked on another troopship bound for Liverpool and demobilisation.

On docking at Liverpool we were informed on the Tannoy that the then prime minister, Clement Attlee, had extended national service from 18 months to 2 years on account of the war in Korea.

So instead of being demobilised, I was ordered to report to Lt General Arbuthnot G.O.C. Highland District at Edinburgh Castle. I was to be attached to the Black Watch depot Queens Barracks Perth. Under Lt. Colonel David Rose the 2nd Battalion BW was being resuscitated for service in Korea. I would not go to Korea as my remaining length of service was too short.

The Black Watch mess was well catered for by the able mess secretary Mr Semple, one of who's preoccupations was deciphering who had what to drink from illegible chits. Resident members of the mess at that time were, Mick Baker Baker, Freddie Burnaby Atkins, Ian Walker, Andy Watson, and others. Also accommodated was my great friend David Lochhead of the Seaforth Highlanders. One distinguished ex service honorary member was Brigadier Bernard Fergusson, who became Lord Ballantrae.

He always wore a monocle even at Eton. He would occasionally drop in to the mess if he was in the area. One of the stories he told against himself was set in pre war India. As a young subaltern he came bouncing into the mess in Delhi one day to proudly announce that he had been invited to the Viceroy's fancy dress ball, did anyone have a suggestion as to what he should go as? Vesey Holt the senior subaltern looked up from his newspaper and said "Dash it, Fergusson, why don't you take off that infernal monocle, stick it up your arse, and go as a telescope!"

Occasionally there were dining in nights. As the most junior officer I sometimes had to act as Mr Vice and respond to the loyal toast by simply saying "The King". Haggis was sometimes served with Mr Semple going round the table pouring copious amounts of whisky over everyone's haggis to the accompaniment of a piper.

One night after such a dinner the dining room was cleared for some all male Scottish reel practice. At one stage, I was whirling visiting Lt General Arbuthnot about when he lost his grip and, being of slight build went crashing across the room and slumped to the floor. He recovered with a good showing of sang froid. It is not often a young subaltern can throw a general across a room and get away with it!

Not long after the London season the Scottish season would start. Grouse shooting started off literally with a bang on 12th August. There were lots of dinner parties, and grand Highland balls calling for white gloves and carnets. I was once asked to hand deliver a thank you note to Primrose Cadogan at Snaigow. The Countess very kindly offered me a pre lunch drink and the opportunity to admire some outstanding Canaletto paintings. Having taken leave of my platoon my national service came to an end and I found myself walking out of Queens Barracks Perth in civilian clothes without ceremony.

Subaltern. Attached to Black Watch depot Queen's barracks Perth.

Little did I know that I would soon be serving part time in the Territorial Army practicing beach landings on the Isle of Wight, followed by 2 years as a civilian FARELF reserve officer in the Malayan Emergency. Finally, in 1956 I served part time with The Royal Hong Kong Regiment in Hong Kong on civil unrest control duties, and Chinese border patrols. These army duties were interspersed with my responsibilities at The HongKong and Shanghai Banking Corporation.

I seem to have collected more military medals for less effort in peace time, than my father did serving in France in WW1. I was never tested in action, so, not surprisingly, non of my medals are for gallantry. Starting with my National Service medal, the rest are merely campaign and commemorative.

Footnote

The Black Watch did go to Korea and were distinguished in the battle of The Hook. For his conduct during fierce hand to hand fighting a BW jock Private Speakman attached to the KOSB was awarded the V C. Lt. William Purves serving with the KOSB was awarded the DSO for his conduct in Korea.

Willie became HSBC Group Chairman, and was deservedly knighted for services to banking.

CHAPTER THREE

The City

In 1951 I had finished my national service and was at a loose end. Arthur Fryers, who worked for HSBC in Hamburg, was on leave in Scotland. He suggested I should consider a career in banking. His stories about pre war life in Shanghai were about junior expatriates being able to afford luxury flats, Russian mistresses, and strings of polo ponies, inspired me to write to HSBC London. As a result, I was invited to be interviewed at the bank by Mr Gray, the senior manager. Following the interview, I received a letter offering me the position of Foreign Staff trainee in London office at a salary of £220 per annum. It was understood that, if I successfully completed my training, I should expect to join the Foreign Staff for service abroad. I accepted the offer. After all, this was no ordinary international bank. This was the real thing! This was THE HONGKONG AND SHANGHAI BANKING CORPORATION. At that time the Bank (HSBC)) could be described as a financial institution, established in 1865, internationally owned, British managed, head quartered in Hong Kong, and having a global network of offices engaged in, inter alia, the profitable finance of foreign trade.

My father was good enough to give me a modest allowance, enabling me to rent a small bed-sit on the top floor of a house in Sloane Street. From time to time London smog was so bad that I, and others, had to light newspapers to see our way down Sloane Street to Sloane Square tube station. I bought myself a slim umbrella (never to be unfurled), and a smart bowler hat from Locks. So armed with these, I thought I would at least look the part of a city learner banker. Then the prospect of a generous pension at a relatively early age was appealing. What impressed me most, however, was the bank's reputation for being an egalitarian meritocracy, unencumbered with nepotism or dynastic considerations. The London office of The Hongkong and Shanghai Banking Corporation was at 9 Gracechurch Street, in the city. Completed in 1913, it had a long banking hall flanked by marble pillars and mahogany counters of generous proportions. Managers offices were at the far end of the banking hall.

These were guarded by the head messenger who had a position outside the senior manager's door. Outward bills department was on the left of the entrance with current accounts and cash departments opposite.

Formal study for the Bankers Institute exams was very much encouraged, as was participation in sport. Rugby was favoured by the Bank as a means of encouraging a culture of team players, rather than dysfunctional prima donnas! To help with my studies I bought a copy of Thomson's dictionary of banking and started a lifelong working habit of reading The Financial Times and The Economist. I believe Thomas Carlyle once said "teach a parrot to say supply and demand, and you have made an economist of him." As part of my training I spent a few weeks in current accounts department. The account ledgers were huge and covered in calf skin. The binding mechanism on the ledgers was ingeniously lockable to allow for secure removal and insertion of numbered pages. A team of clerks, some wearing green eye shades and arm bands, would post the transactions using pen and ink. At night the ledgers were locked away in the book safe and taken out again the next working morning. The Chartered Bank was the arch rival of HSBC. In jest it was said that Chartered Bank staff were bankers trying to be gentlemen whereas HSBC staff were gentlemen trying to be bankers! Another part of my training was an assignment to outward bills department. This department dealt with documents relating to export letters of credit. Despite being very busy, the department head was good enough to take time to explain various aspects of the work to the trainees. The names and addresses of the beneficiaries of o/b department settlement cheques had to be hand written on printed covering letters. The names and addresses then had to be written again on the envelopes for posting. To save double work I had the non brainer to suggest that we should use window envelopes. I was pleased to see my suggestion adopted. One of my duties in o/b was to keep the heated sealing wax pot filled. Sealing wax was put on documentary mail packets on which the bank's seal was impressed. I was also responsible for writing up some settlement cheques, enumerating l/c documents such as bills of lading and insurance certificates. Occasionally we were required to work overtime for an hour or two, and were given half a crown for our trouble. In my case, my payment was usually accompanied by a request to get a hair cut. P J Wodehouse once worked for the bank. It is said that one day he felt overwhelmed with paper work. In order to reduce his work load he deliberately dropped a pile of documents from his desk over London Bridge. By chance the documents landed on a barge passing below. The documents were duly handed in to the bank, resulting in PJW's ignominious departure. David Heneage, (the Baron). an unlikely FS trainee, caused a bit of a stir amongst the staff. He often enacted the role of a sort of super snob, who frequently described people who he thought beneath him socially, as guttersnipes. One day a Chinese customer came into the bank at about 3pm, at which time we were allowed to smoke. The customer was greeted at the counter by the Baron who, blowing smoke from his long amber cigarette holder into the customers face, patronisingly asked, "What do you want?" The customer said he wanted to see Mr Gray, the manager. The Baron then called out to the head messenger "Tell Mr Gray there is a tired little oriental number to see him." Unfortunately for the Baron, the customer turned out to be a highly respected knighted Hong Kong taipan. The Baron didn't last too long at the Bank. Surprisingly, when he left his colleagues chipped in and gave him a farewell party at a city pub. He was genuinely missed. At a luncheon party given by Lady Jessica Forres at her house in St Johns Wood, she asked me if I could sponsor her youngest son Angus to join the Bank. I was happy to do this, knowing that the family firm, Balfour Williamson, was one of the bank's tenants at 9 Gracechurch Street. The Hon. Angus was duly taken on, but I'm afraid, he didn't find banking much to his liking, and departed after a short time.

After work, I was occasionally invited to dinner at the Bank of England. My great friend Michael Shurey was doing his national service in the Coldstream Guards. Occasionally he was on duty as piquet officer guarding the Bank of England. As such he was allowed one male dinner guest. Dinner was served in very grand surroundings by a white gloved butler. I'm afraid at that time we were not sophisticated enough to do justice to the treasures of the BOE wine cellar.

Far from being rich and blue blooded, I was surprised to find myself tagged on to the list of male eligibles invited to the season's Deb coming out dances. There must have been a shortage of men. It would have been amusing, at that time, to have been able to boast, in jest, about an imaginative Debrettish ancestor. Perhaps a made up name like

Egbert the Pilferer, a medieval banker, might have impressed the girl's mums. The cost of hiring white tie and tails from Moss Bros. was at least offset by the free dinners, sometimes before, and sometimes at the dance venues. On a good evening one could dine gratis at Claridges or Quaglinos and, on a really good evening, end up as someone's guest at The 400. I became a member of The Cafe de Paris Guinea Pig Club. As such, I enjoyed affordable cabaret and dancing evenings for the young with more dash than cash. Noel Coward, Victor Borge, and Marlene Dietrich, were some of the memorable cabaret performers.

The **TATLER** & **BYSTANDER**

Vol. CCIV. No. 2654
TWO SHILLINGS   Postage: Inland 2d.   Canada 1½d.   Foreign 2½d.

MAY 21
1952

The débutantes, all dressed in white, descend the stairway to make their curtsy

Queen Charlotte's Ball
Introduced The Season

OVER one thousand guests gathered at the Grosvenor House Hotel to be present at Queen Charlotte's Ball, the "coming-out" for many of this year's débutantes. Highlight of the evening was the young girls' parade down the stairway to make their curtsy before the giant birthday cake, while after the ceremony the young people, together with their parents and friends, continued dancing until the early hours of the morning. On the right, Miss Bridget Brew is partnered in a foxtrot by Mr. John Ledingham. More pictures of the occasion on pages 416 and 417

The TATLER and Bystander, May 21, 1952

Continuing——

PRELUDE TO A SHINING
SEASON FOR DÉBUTANTES

FIRST of many important occasions for 1952 débutantes was Queen Charlotte's Ball, given annually in honour of the birthday of the consort of King George III. Later in the season the débutantes will again make a curtsy—to H.M. Queen Elizabeth—at Buckingham Palace or Holyroodhouse. Jennifer gives a full description of this impressive Ball on pages 425 and 426

Miss Joan Shedden, Miss Mary Orr Deas and Miss Jill Archer, three of the maids of honour, were in company with Mr. J. A. Smith

One of the most charming débutantes was Miss Jacynth Lindsay, daughter of Mr. Martin Lindsay, D.S.O., M.P. for Solihull, Warwickshire, and Mrs. Lindsay. She wore a dress of broderie anglaise trimmed with pink roses

Mr. John Money escorted Miss Jennifer Cameron, who comes from Yorkshire

Countess Waldegrave chatted with Margherita, Lady Howard de Walden, President of the Ball

Miss Huguette Gordon and Mr. Martin Cowling took time off from the dance floor to watch from a balcony

Mr. Richard Brew discussed the cabaret, an exhibition of ballroom dancing, with Miss Judith Hancock

Enjoying a waltz together before dinner was served were Miss Angela Dodd and Mr. James Dodd

Miss Marilyn Hartley, daughter of Mr. Lister Hartley, the golfer, and Mrs. Hartley, was partnered by Mr. John Lyle-Purdy

The TATLER and Bystander, MAY 21, 1952
417

In conference were the Hon. Julia Blunt-Mackenzie, daughter of Viscount Tarbat, Miss Barbara Houison-Crawfurd and Miss Gillian Grant, who all live in Scotland

Relaxing for a few minutes with cigarettes were Mr. Christopher Talbot, Miss Daphne Hudson and Mr. Sandy McCardle, while chatting together were Miss Margaret King-Farlow and Mr. Michael Shurey

Studying the programme were Miss Jacqueline Hewitt, from New York, Miss Jane Graves and Miss Christine Fergusson

Miss Mary Glyn discussed the list of events with Mr. Jeremy Glyn, while Mr. Robin Bridgeman also took an interest in the proceedings

The débutantes make their curtsy to the cake. Illuminated by 200 candles, it was cut by the chief guest, Her Grace the Duchess of Roxburghe, who afterwards presented a piece to each of the maids of honour.

Deb's delight?

Reg Ives the paternal London office accountant, was good enough to approve an unsecured overdraft limit of £100 for me. Despite that, I still had to look to my father as lender of last resort! God knows how many lectures I had to endure about having to live within my means. I remember, a joke doing the rounds, was about "The sex worker trying to make ends meet!"

I enjoyed cockney humour, such as the two notices on an east end pub. One read "Please don't ask for credit, he doesn't work here anymore!" The other notice read, "Please don't ask for credit, 'cos a smack on the mouth might cause offence!"

Another story was about the cockney couple who had won a fortune on the football pools. The missus said that they should use some of the money to educate the kids. So their two boys were packed off to Eton. On arrival, their housemaster told them to write to their parents with a list of clothes they would need. Their father was none too pleased at the cost of all the clothes. When the clothes arrived, the housemaster told the boys to write to their mater and pater thanking them. The boys wrote" dear Mum and Dad, Ta for the clobber. We're running around 'ere like a couple of counts." On reading the letter, the old man exclaimed, "Blimey, all that dosh on education, and they can't even spell!"

A minor item on my then embryonic bucket list, was to climb the 300 stairs of The Monument. I managed to do it effortlessly on my lunch hour one day. This brings to mind Oscar Wilde's epigram about youth being wasted on the young.

I usually had lunch in the Bank canteen, not least because it was free. Given that there is no such thing as a free lunch, I suppose it was really part of ones emoluments. Occasionally, I would splash out and have a snack lunch and a glass of wine at the well known Jamaica wine house, just round the corner from the Bank. A stroll around Leadenhall market was always interesting.

Sweets were still rationed in 1952. John Gray and I became the office sweet coupon brokers. In this way we were able to facilitate the hard up office girls selling their sweet coupons to others. Not a very profitable pastime, but at least we were never short of a mars bar.

I have only been shot at once. It happened outside a high rise block of flats near Marble Arch. The would be assassin was Tim who was at Stowe with my friend Michael Shurey. Tim did not find his national service in the RAF to his liking, and as a deserter turned up in London. Michael Shurey who was living in the mess at Wellington Barracks, gave Tim his room in his father's Mayfair flat, the father being away in the South of France. Tim was also given a luger pistol, one of many brought back from Germany by Michael's nco's. So there was a bizarre scenario of a serving army officer harbouring an armed deserter.

Unfortunately, Shurey senior returned unexpectedly from France to find Tim in his bed with a floozie. The pair were ejected from the flat in very short order. Undaunted Tim and the floozie booked in to the Dorchester hotel, paying the bill with a forged cheque drawn on his father's account. Tim's father had been the proprietor of the Shanghai Morning Post, nationalised by the communists in 1948 without compensation. On leaving the Dorchester the pair then rented a flat in Duke Street St. James. Once again a forged cheque was used to pay the rent. I was invited to a drinks party at the Duke Street flat, and arrived just in time to witness Tim fire a shot from his luger harmlessly into the ceiling. At a subsequent party in Marble Arch Tim was hopelessly drunk. He unjustly accused me of stealing his girl friend. He then proceeded to stub out a cigarette on the back of his hand to prove his love for the girl. The girl told him not to be so stupid and asked me to take her home. We had just about reached my car when three shots rang out from above. All the shots missed. To this day I can still hear the sound of the bullets ricocheting. Tim having a burned hand, alcohol fuelled, and high up in the dark, we were, mercifully, not easy targets.

Some years later when I was accountant in Bangkok, Tim turned up at the office. I was too busy to talk to him, so I asked him to stay the night with us and suggested we meet at The Two Vikings, an up market Bangkok restaurant, for dinner. At the end of the month I received a colossal bill for the dinner. It seems Tim had arrived at the restaurant three hours early. The bill was mostly for the expensive cocktail chits he had signed on my account. In due course he married a rich American lady with similar tastes. Rumours are strongly denied they kept Johnny Walker in overtime. Sadly Tim died while swimming in the Caribbean.

I also acquired one of Michael Shurey's luger pistols. Years later I sold it to a colleague in Hong Kong on his posting to Bangkok. Unfortunately he was arrested in Cambodia for attempting to smuggle out prohibited artefacts. Humphrey had been in the habit of making weekend excursions to Cambodia to find and bring back antique stone carved Buddha heads, even though the practice was prohibited. One weekend he and two Embassy girls were caught at the border trying to take some Buddha heads illegally out of Cambodia. In a custody cell with the two girls Humphrey was trying to ram the luger into the knickers of one of the girls in the belief that she would have diplomatic immunity and would not be searched. Alas, the girl would have non of it, and poor old Humphrey was charged with, not only trying to smuggle out Buddha heads, but also possessing an unlicensed gun. He was incarcerated in Cambodia, in grim circumstances, for some time before his release.

In the summer of 1952 I found myself, with others, at a burgeoning bottle party at Fleur Kirwin Taylor's London flat. As the evening progressed more and more people arrived carrying everything from vintage Krug to Blue Nun. At one stage I was talking to Fleur in the kitchen when Denholm Elliott a budding actor, barged in. He obviously took an instant inebriated dislike to me, and launched a full bottle of milk in my direction. It missed and smashed messily against a tiled wall. The assailant, sensing my retaliatory fury, wisely fled the scene.

The whole country was plunged into mourning when the King died in February 1952. Somehow, everyone in London office managed to find something black to wear. The men wearing black ties or armbands. Not long afterwards, I received my orders to join the Foreign Staff and proceed to Hong Kong.

CHAPTER FOUR

Singapore

Arrangements were made for me to share a first class cabin with Peter Parsons on the P&O liner Chusan. Peter and I were Foreign Staff contemporaries and were on friendly terms.

Apart from a paucity of attractive female company, the voyage was pleasant enough. Lots of reading, deck sports, and, of course, dressing for dinner. I soon found myself in the pretentious habit of enjoying a large cigar and a brandy after dinner. There was on board an HSBC senior manager en route to Jakarta after leave. At Port Said he persuaded me to join him scouring the back streets for pornographic post cards. My senior colleague was delighted when we eventually found some. Years later I reminded him of our adventure when he was visiting Japan on internal audit. The ship had just left Bombay when I received a telegram with orders to disembark at Singapore. It seemed that someone in the Bank in Singapore had broken a leg playing rugby. I was to be his supernumerary replacement. This was a huge disappointment for me as I was looking forward to seeing all my friends in Hong Kong.

I much enjoyed working in Singapore. My job in cash department at the Collyer Quay office of the bank was not too onerous. I had an American car and an American girlfriend who was the daughter

29

of the head of Firestone in Singapore. She and I spent the evening of the Queen's Coronation driving round the Maidan watching the celebrations before going on to a black tie dinner dance at a popular night spot. I was dancing with her when a huge black spider fell from the ceiling on to my shoulder and started to crawl up my neck. I instinctively brushed it off with some force. The thing flew across the dance floor and landed on the leg of a woman seated on a chair. Pandemonium broke out. Luckily, someone grabbed a dinner plate and squashed the spider dead on the woman's leg.

Life in Singapore carried on, with lots of swimming and tennis at the Tanglin club and on our own court at Sri Menanti. Early morning riding at Bukit Timah and weekends at the bank's holiday bungalow in Loyang with my girl friend were much enjoyed. It came as a shock to me when I was summoned to the accountant's office to be told I was posted to Penang, with immediate effect. This was to be one of the many short notice moves the bank required of me over the years.

CHAPTER FIVE

Singapore to Penang 1953

Having made my farewells I decided to drive to Penang. Somehow I managed to pack all my possessions into the car. The most difficult things to fit in were my camphor wood chest and a glass acid carboy. I used the carboy as a lamp base. All that done I set off at about 5 AM and was soon over the causeway into Johore Bahru. Driving through endless rubber trees was quite an eerie experience. In the half light of dawn, one could be forgiven for imagining a communist terrorist lurking in ambush behind every tree. There was absolutely no one on the road, and I was able to keep up a good pace until I arrived at Muar. The ferry across the Muar river was an antiquated flat barge like contraption, winched back and forth by ropes. I did not stop at Muar as I was anxious to reach Ipoh before dark. Interestingly, the bank had a small office in Muar. It was once rumoured that the foreign staff bachelor in charge preferred the company of his girl friend in bed rather than sitting around in the afternoon in his office below his flat. Apparently he had the ingenious, if not licentious, idea of creating a trapdoor by his bedside, so that anything he had to sign could be sent up and down by the compradore on a pulley with a warning bell attached. I am not sure conducting banking in this way would have had the approval of everyone in Head Office!

I was able to refuel at Serembam, where a Gurkha officer told me my route ahead was well patrolled and should be free from trouble, ominously adding, "but you never know!" I was reminded of the expression "So far so good, as the man said jumping off the skyscraper!" Both Generals Templar and (later) Bourne deserve much credit for defeating the Communist Terrorists in what was a long campaign in Malaya. On the road I was comforted by my Luger pistol kept handy in the glove box. The possession of an unlicensed gun during the emergency in Malaya carried the death penalty. Despite that, I could never quite bring myself to part with the gun. As a FARELF reserve officer I hoped my unlicensed weapon would be condoned. Thank goodness, this defensive piece of wishful thinking was never tested. I eventually left Malaya unchallenged with the gun intact.

I arrived in Kuala Lumpur in good time for some delicious Dutch pea soup and a curry at the Selangor club. During lunch I was able to watch some Fijian soldiers playing rugby in white pointed skirts with bare feet! I paid a courtesy call on the Kula Lumpur manager before heading off to the alluvial tin mining town of Ipoh. The manager of Ipoh office and his wife were kind enough to put me up for the night. I'm afraid the wife was in a very distraught state because of her paranoid fear of communist terrorists. All the shutters of the house were kept permanently closed to give the poor woman some comfort. Thanking my hosts, I set off early next morning. I had a refuelling stop, accompanied by some roadside nasi goring, and a tiger beer, before arriving at the Butterworth ferry.

As soon as I arrived in Penang, I was given a roasting on the telephone from the accountant in Singapore, for not having made the journey by ship for safety reasons. My excuse was that I was never told that I was meant to travel by sea. My excuse was accepted, and I was grudgingly congratulated on having made the trip unharmed. I was even allowed to claim reimbursement for my petrol expenses, having unwittingly saved the bank the cost of a sea passage.

PENANG

On arriving at the office, I was told the reason for my transfer from Singapore was the result of a colleague having a nervous breakdown. He was still living in the bachelor mess awaiting an escort for a passage to Blighty. There was no vacant accommodation for me in the mess, so I had to make do with a makeshift bed made up on an upstairs verandah. There was one occasion, whilst in bed, during a tropical storm, I found myself looking straight into the hypnotic glistening eyes of a gibbon sheltering in a palm tree close to the verandah, only a few feet from my face. One morning the mentally disturbed colleague I was replacing came down to breakfast, grabbed a kitchen knife and ran screaming in to the adjacent jungle. Eventually he was found, brought back, and sedated by a doctor. He was fit enough to depart the next day, allowing me to have my own room at last. We were all very sorry to see him go in such sad circumstances.

I was put in charge of the current accounts department of the bank. I was fortunate to have a good team of clerks, nearly all were Hokien Chinese. One of whom turned out to be a world champion badminton player. He was often away on special leave to play matches all over the world. The annual Haj of the Muslims to Mecca was a busy time for the office. The faithful would come off ships from Indonesia, and elsewhere, in their thousands and queue outside the bank. At these times it was all hands to the pump to deal with the issue of travellers cheques demand drafts, money changing, and telegraphic transfers. The main business of the branch was commercial letters of credit covering exports and imports. On the export side, rubber and smelted tin were the main commodities. Imports covered everything from cars to cribs. Social life varied, from the Piccadilly Dance Hall to the semi exclusiveness of the Penang Club. The Runnymede Hotel was the preserve of wives of the armed forces. The Lone Pine hotel was a short coastal drive from the town. The E&O hotel, with it's whispering gallery, was in the town centre. Occasionally, I was detailed to make army escorted cash runs to our office in Sungai Petani. These trips were almost all trouble free. The cash was delivered to pay army and rubber plantation workers. The latter were mostly Tamils from South India. I flew down to Singapore from time to time to see my American girl friend. Alas, her father was transferred to the U S A thus effectively ending our romance. I was enjoying my work and playing lots of tennis when, unexpectedly, the Bank ordered me, again at short notice, to proceed to Kuala Lumpur.

CHAPTER SIX

Kuala Lumpur

I packed up my belongings in my American Nash car and headed for Kuala Lumpur. This time, I was careful to join an army escorted convoy and duly arrived in the capital safely.

The mess was a relatively modern bungalow situated off the Ipoh road about a mile from the city centre. Being the most junior, I was allocated an un air conditioned bedroom. The en suite bathroom had a loo and washbasin but no bath or shower. It did have a Shanghai jar kept topped up with water by the house boy. The idea was that, using a saucepan, one would pour water all over ones self, use the soap, and then finish by pouring more water to remove the soap. On a visit by the Chief Manager Sir Michael Turner, I was grateful to his wife Wendy who insisted that my bedroom should be air conditioned and that a proper shower should be provided in the bathroom. Lady Turner also had the kitchen updated with the provision of a new refrigerator. Prior to that, the cook would buy live fish in the market. The fish would be kept live in a pail until cooked and eaten. Chickens were attached live to the stove by string until needed. The thinking was, if it's alive it's fresh!

Shortly after my arrival in KL I spent an agonising week dragging myself to the office feeling absolutely wretched with a temperature and excruciating bad back pain. In the end I was forced to see the doctor who told me I had just experienced a bad attack of dengue fever. I was ordered to bed over the weekend and was back in the office much recovered on Monday morning. At about the same time I developed a skin problem on my hands. The cause was the red dye coming off the current account cheques on to my hands. As head of current accounts department I played a pivotal role in the processing of customer's cheque books drawn on the bank. One of my duties was to examine cheque books before they were posted in the hand written ledgers. A decision to return a cheque unpaid could be made for a number of reasons. Such as:

Post dated, out of date, no date, words and figures differ, no words, insufficient funds, cheque mutilated, signature not in accordance with specimen, payment countermanded, and so on. Spotting a good forgery was almost impossible. As a security measure, customers were advised to keep their cheque books under lock and key. Unlike Singapore and Penang, K L office was not air conditioned. There was usually an uncomfortable degree of humidity, and papers had to be weighted against being blown about by the overhead fans.

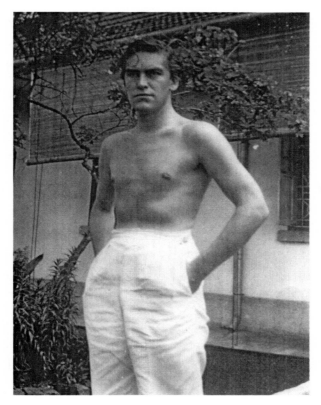

Convalescent. Recuperating from dengue fever. Kula Lumpur 1955.

Following a decision to mechanise current accounts the NCR postronic machines arrived and we began the changeover after banking hours. All went well until we tried to balance. We were unable to balance. Working night after night, often till after midnight, we were all mystified as to why we could not balance the ledgers against the journals. With the help of NCR we finally discovered that one of the machine operators had not cleared his machine before starting a run. To cover his mistake he had rolled back the proof backing sheet and overprinted the cleared symbol on an uncleared figure in the machine. The uncleared figure turned out to be the same amount of the balance discrepancy. The culprit was one of the Indian clerical staff who posted the journals. Understandably, he was not very popular for a time.

One weekend we were all surprised in the mess when a colleague emptied a sack of human bones on the ante room floor. He had been exploring the Batu Caves near Ipoh and had found the skeleton. There was much speculation about the skeleton. Some of us thought it might be that of a Japanese soldier but no one could be sure. The bones were handed in to the police, but nothing more was heard.

On another weekend, Harry Lee, my Scottish colleague, and I were invited to a rubber plantation for curry lunch. After a very boozy lunch we decided to drive home before dark in Harry's large Humber car. On the plantation dirt road through a patch of jungle Harry swerved either to kill or dodge a snake. The car plunged off the road and started to sink rapidly in a swamp.

The water pressure prevented us from opening the doors. Our life's were undoubtedly saved by our being able to escape through the hand operated sun roof. The last sign we saw of the car was some bubbles appearing through the slimy green water of the swamp. On another occasion Harry and I were invited to a drinks party at the Selangor club. On the way we stopped at Nantos Milk Bar for some cigarettes. Nantos, was a very rough pub and was a favourite hangout of army other ranks. It was certainly not a Milk Bar. Dressed in a tie and tropical suit I made my way through the crowd towards the bar. A drunken soldier took a dislike to me and barred my way. Push came to shove resulting in a full scale fist fight. Before I knew it, I was being punched and kicked from all sides, ending up being thrown outside into the monsoon drain. Harry, who was waiting in the car, came to my assistance. On reaching the Selangor club I was able to tidy myself up in the cloak room and proceeded in to drinks. On meeting the Lindsay sisters I apologised for my disheveled appearance. Their father was on General Templar's staff.

Not too long afterwards I was on a night out with two army friends.

Patrick Cleland SAS and Timothy Heneage 7th Hussars. We were driving back to the HSBC mess for a night cap when my Nash left the road.

The car catapulted down and crashed nose first through the tiled roof of an empty outhouse some distance below. I recall having a brief surreal feeling of flying. We were all left hanging upside down in the car. Fortunately no one was seriously injured. At my desk the next morning, covered in cuts and bruises, and with a monumental hangover, I pondered on where on earth I had left the car the night before. Mike Holmden, the acting manager, came up to my desk and, in conversation, casually mentioned that a car had come off the cliff and crashed through the roof of his outhouse. He was more than surprised when I sheepishly confessed to being the driver. Sadly, not too long after, Mike Holmden was to die of a heart attack while walking on Lama island Hong Kong in 1960.

Timothy Heneage told me that on one occasion he had to take out all the cooks, drivers and clerks in his unit just to show them what the jungle was like. In the jungle, against all odds, they suddenly came across a CT camp. Amid LOUD shouts of "keep quiet!" and the din of rifle bolts rattling, the rookie patrol charged the CT's, amazingly killing two of them.

Patrick Cleland spent many weeks away after parachuting in to the jungle. He never talked about his experiences.

I vividly remember a hair raising experience on a jungle road outside Kuala Lumpur. I had to swerve to avoid a child. In doing so I clipped a row of poles supporting a row of roadside attap houses. Unfortunately some of the houses came down and I was chased by some very angry villagers armed with parangs. I had the presence of mind to throw some dollars out of the car window. This had the desired effect of diverting the would be assassins and, at the same time, giving them some compensation.

With about a year to go before the end of my first tour, I was ordered to report to Hong Kong. I was told to proceed to Singapore and from there take a ship to Hong Kong. I was given a highly confidential letter to be hand delivered to Mike Sandberg the Singapore accountant. I duly handed over the letter, and enjoyed a tiger beer with him in his house in the Bank's Sri Menanti compound. I was not privy to the contents of the letter. I had an idea it was something to do with the Bank's contingency plans concerning the approaching independence of Malaya.

CHAPTER SEVEN

Hong Kong

As a newly arrived foreign staff junior in Hong Kong, I was occasionally assigned to be in charge of "the diamond trade". This meant going down to a large secure walk in safe in the bank's basement. Here there was a table covered with a black velvet cloth. On this cloth packets of cut polished diamonds would be opened and the contents spread out for selection by one or other of the leading Hong Kong jewellers. Each packet was sent by secure post from our correspondent bank usually Mees and Hope in Holland. The customer would choose which stones they liked and were allowed to take them against payment. The annual turnover of diamond sales in Hong Kong was huge. The business was profitable to the bank who charged the customer a handling fee. A commission was also charged to the customer AND the remitting bank on the sale. Additionally there was always the exchange profit between HK $'s and the settlement currency. So all in all this highly profitable business was considered "quite satisfactory "My main job was to process documents and bills drawn under the terms of documentary irrevocable import letters of credit opened for our customers. Typically a customer would import bales of raw cotton and would sometimes ask for a loan against the security of the raw cotton deposited in our godown (warehouse). The customer would then pay for the release of raw cotton to go to the cotton mills for spinning into cotton yarn. The yarn would be converted into manufactured-piece goods for export under an export letter of credit. Export letters of credit would sometimes have a "red" clause guaranteeing a packing credit loan. Against the proceeds of the export credit, the customer would open another import letter of credit and the whole process would be repeated over and over again. This business was highly profitable to the bank. Not only was there commission income, but storage and handling charges, as well as foreign exchange profit and loan interest. The short term nature of the loans suited our liquidity constraints.

On my first arrival in Hong Kong I was introduced to the two bronze lions Stephen and Stit who guarded the entrance to the bank at 1 Queen's Road Central. The lions were first installed in the 1920's and named after two managers of the time. During the Japanese occupation in WW2 the lions were viewed by the Japanese as a symbol of British imperialism and were removed to Japan to be melted down. Amazingly, just after the war the lions were found in a scrap yard in Japan. They were brought back to Hong Kong and reinstalled and can be seen guarding the Bank to-day.

I spent many happy times trawling for antiques in Cat Street and Hollywood Road. I recall having my shirts made by Mee Yee in Wellington Street. Concealed front buttons, large monogrammed breast pocket, french cuffs, waisted and with a generous tail together with provision for collar stiffeners were, for me, basic requirements. I often chose Japanese Kanebo silk. My amah hated this fabric, so difficult to iron!

In 1956 serious rioting erupted in Hong Kong. A few of us, in the Bank, volunteered to serve part time in The Royal Hong Kong Regiment. For some reason I mostly found myself man handling maxim machine guns up and down the Kowloon hills close to the Chinese border. During rioting a Swiss couple tragically became trapped in their car and were burned to death. Eventually the civil unrest abated and, in January 1957, I was granted eight months leave having completed my first tour of four years.

CHAPTER EIGHT

Leave 1957

I decided to take a Pan Am flight from Hong Kong to London via Rome and Paris. At that time flying was still a novel mode of transport and the bank allowed all seniorities to fly first class. That luxury for everyone didn't last too long. Junior staff soon found themselves at the back of the aeroplane. It would be some years before the airlines introduced business class travel.

Being young, and status conscious, I was not pleased to be told in Rome that I was being downgraded to economy for the connecting flight to Paris. The reason for this was that the new aircraft was on an inaugural flight from Rome to New York, and all first class seats were reserved for the occasion. Since Pan Am made no attempt to offer any compensation, I decided never to fly with Pan Am again.

Travellor's Letter of Credi. Fore runner of the credit card.

I checked in to the Maurice hotel in Paris. I was slightly disappointed to find they had given me a room with oriental decor. I would have much preferred more of a French ambience. In any case, I lost no time in heading out to sample some Parisian nightlife. My alcohol fuelled lost weekend ended with three Algerians taking my watch and travellers cheques at knife point. I reported the incident to the police. They simply shrugged, and said it happens all the time. Over lunch I reported the loss of my travellers cheques to the HSBC Paris manager in his impressive Place Vendome panelled office. After paying my hotel bill for three unused nights, I caught a BEA flight to London.

Arriving in London I shared a small house in Kinnerton Street with my friend Michael Shurey. I bought my first Rolls Royce with the registration plate DOM 11. Not long after I bought the car, I attended a coming out dance for Patricia Rawlings and Susan Douglas at Claridges. On leaving the hotel, I was just about to drive off when a policeman politely tipped his helmet and enquired if I was sober enough to drive! I said I was, and promptly drove round the corner grazing a lamp post. Thankfully, I was out of sight of the bobby. I drove on to Kinnerton street with thick acrid smoke coming from where, after the collision, my front mudguard was pressed on to the tyre. The next morning a few of us decided to drive to Paris. On arrival in Paris, Nick Embiricos elected to stay with his uncle while the rest of us found rooms in a hotel on the Champs Elysees. At a shipboard party given by Norman Butler on the Queen Mary in Southampton, the Rolls suffered yet another mishap. I was reversing on the quay and did not see a low rise solid iron bollard. The boot was damaged preventing the girls in the party from retrieving their overcoats. There followed much recrimination. I spent some time with my family in Scotland, and drove north as far as Cape Wrath in the Rolls, tout en famille.

Towards the end of my leave I received orders to proceed to Tokyo. The Rolls was sold back to the dealer, at a loss, before my departure for Japan.

CHAPTER NINE

Japan

It was arranged that I would proceed to Japan by P&O liner. On this voyage I had my own first class cabin.

On reaching Port Said I joined an excursion to see the pyramids and stay overnight at Gisa. We arrived in Gisa after dark. I was given a spacious room in the Mena House Hotel. When the attendant opened the jalousies I was treated to the unforgettable sight of the pyramids and the Sphinx bathed in moon light, only a stones throw away. Very early next morning we were all mounted on camels and proceeded to the Cheops pyramid. In those days we were allowed to crawl through a very narrow claustrophobic passage on hands and knees into the burial chamber. Despite the discomfort, it was a memorable experience, and worthy of a tick on my bucket list. The ship stopped briefly to pick us up at a Red Sea rendezvous after the Suez Canal. Our next port of call was Aden in the Yemen. I joined a shore excursion and enjoyed seeing the camel market and a lake covered with thousands of pink flamingos.

On shore at Bombay we were persuaded to watch an arranged fight to the death between a mongoose and a king cobra. It wasn't much of a contest. The agile mongoose soon made short work of the snake. On shore in Colombo I had a swim at Breach Kandy followed by tea at the Galle Face Hotel. Mrs Bandaranaike, the wife of Ceylon's prime minister, came on board on her way to Singapore.

I disembarked in Singapore and boarded an RIL cargo passenger ship en route to Japan. The ship conveniently berthed in Hong Kong for two days en route. In Hong Kong I paid a courtesy call on senior managers in the Bank, some of whom gave me a few tips on what to expect in Japan.

Any notion of Japan being about cherry blossom and kimonos was quickly dispelled on my arrival in Kobe harbour. Looking out of my cabin porthole, all I could see were factory chimneys belching forth mostly yellow acrid smoke. There were men in hard hats wandering around wearing strange foot ware with separate compartments for big toes.

A foreign staff colleague from Kobe office came on board and said that Tokyo office would like me to disembark and proceed to Tokyo by bullet train. It was felt it would be a waste of time for me to take another two days to disembark at Yokohama.

Although Japan was occupied by US forces, the sight of a non Japanese in Japan was a curiosity at that time. On arrival at Tokyo station I was assailed by students wanting to practice English. Eventually, they found me a taxi to take me to the Tokyo office of the bank.

To a large extent my bachelor social life in Tokyo was influenced by "The Magnificent Seven". They were all young attractive women who's fathers were diplomats in the Tokyo circuit. The doyen of the bevy was Mimi MacArthur daughter of the American Ambassador, followed by Blanca Vilaceros daughter of the Spanish Ambassador, Dominique, Veriot daughter of the French Commercial Councillor, Maria and Graziana Zele daughters of the Italian Naval Military and Airforce attaché, Nicki Chilton daughter of the British Naval attaché, and Elizabeth Mayall daughter of the British Embassy minister. Elizabeth's father, Lees Mayall went on to become Marshall of the Diplomatic Corps and was knighted.

Amongst others in our group were two junior American naval officers Alvin Ward Smith and Bill Post Owen, David Waterstone British Embassy 1st secretary, Kai Falkman a Swedish Embassy attaché and two Dutch nationals from RIL Aak van Steenbergen and Willem Mullock Houwer. So we were certainly cosmopolitan if nothing else.

I was invited to be an usher at Mimi MacArthur's wedding to Alvin Ward Smith in 1960.

The wedding was to take place in the American Embassy and would coincide with a state visit of President Eisenhower. As ushers, we were in the embassy rehearsing the night before the wedding and had the privilege of having a peek at the President's bedroom complete with his and her bathrooms en suite. Unfortunately, that night the militant Japanese Union the zenrokyo had organised a noisy protest outside the embassy. Presidential aide Hagarty flew in by helicopter and, after assessing the situation, cancelled the President's visit. So I was disappointed not to meet President Eisenhower who would have attended the wedding.

Usher with guest at Mimi MacArthur's wedding.
American Embassy Tokyo 1960.

Almost every night there was a diplomatic reception of one sort or another. On some of these occasions I met Princess Chichibu a member of the imperial royal family. She combined intelligence with a great sense of humour. I was always so pleased when she spoke to me.

Riding guest at the Imperial Palace Tokyo

At Elizabeth Mayall's birthday party at the British Embassy I found myself in an altercation (over a woman) with the son of the Turkish Ambassador. After a time we went outside to settle the matter. The Turk was a daunting opponent. He was thick set, muscular and practiced karate every day.

Push came to shove and just as we were about to square up, my bank colleague Billy Hargroves picked up a champagne bottle (full) and felled the Turk, whereupon we made our excuses and departed for the Ginza. We went to a well known night spot where the topless waitresses wore cellophane knickers with a match scratching strip on the back. The idea was for the waitress to bend over while you lit a match, a sort of "lucky strike!".

Unfortunately I stretched my arms and cut my hand rather badly on a low hung ceiling fan. Thereafter the evening passed in a fog of alcohol.

The next thing I knew I was outdoors sliding along a department store window at dawn on Sunday morning, clutching a half empty bottle with my suit covered in blood from my hand injury. Not the evening I had planned. The next day I was shocked to learn that the ambassador father of the Turk had committed suicide.

Perhaps the worst hangover experience I had was after a stag night out for a groom to be. I woke up naked and freezing on a cold marble slab being bitten by mosquitoes. In the pitch dark I had the surreal feeling I was dead and in a morgue. I soon realised I was in a Yokohama bath house which had closed for the night and simply left me out cold on the marble slab. Somehow or other I managed to find my clothes in the dark, break out, and hail a taxi.

In Tokyo at that time it was possible to rent a tramcar complete with jazz band for parties while going round the Tokyo tramlines. We often did this. Sometimes we had to diplomatically repel well meaning over friendly Japanese who wanted to board and join in.

My social life could be described as Jekyll and Hyde.

Typically part of an evening could be spent in the rarefied atmosphere and protocol of the diplomatic world followed later by a tour of the rough G I bars of Yokohama. Graffiti in the bars was amazing. For example "Donald Duck is a Jew" was one of the more printable ones. Japan was still occupied and Tokyo was crammed with GI's on R and R from Korea. About this time my American cousin Major Chuck Sinclair US marines was killed in action in Korea. From time to time a flat top (aircraft carrier) would visit Yokohama and disgorge up to 3000 sailors loaded with dollars all intent on a good time in the bars. Such an event was much to the annoyance of the local patrons.

I'm afraid I found it difficult to appreciate some aspects of Japanese culture. Bunraku Kabuki, and Noh plays all left me unenthused. On the other hand I appreciated Japanese gardens hugely. One of my favourites being the seasonal river of irises in the Meiji gardens. I also enjoyed visits to Kyoto, Atami, Nara, and a few skiing weekends at Shiga Heights.

The autumnal colours at Karuizawa were absolutely outstanding.

Belleisle.

Desmond Fitzgerald The Knight of Glynn stayed with me for a spell in Tokyo. He was searching for good Japanese works of art at the behest of his Canadian step father. It was through Desmond that I first took an interest in antiques. Sadly at that time my spare cash went on Ginza night clubbing rather than antique collecting.

At about this same time my friend Martin Parsons and his brother Brendan visited Tokyo. I arranged for Martin to meet me after work so that I could show him something of the Ginza. That evening the worst typhoon ever hit Tokyo. The wind and rain was so intense the imperial moat overflowed.

Whilst we were vainly trying to hail a taxi we saw huge carp from the overflowing moat attempting to swim along the flooded tram lines and street gutters of Marunouchi. So our planned evening on the town proved to be a non event. I next saw Martin at his wedding to Aline in London where I was introduced to his step brother's wife Princess Margaret. I had met Tony Armstrong Jones, as he then was, much earlier. I was with my then fiancé Wendy Power's friend Janie Baker. We were collecting a collage of photographs from Tony AJ who was living with Jackie Chan in Pimlico at the time. I seem to remember he suddenly emerged out of a secret panel into the room in which we were waiting. Years later Martin's brother Brendan, who had succeeded his father to become the Earl of Rosse, invited Marianne and I to a hugely enjoyable catch up lunch at Birr castle, the family seat in Ireland.

By and large the Japanese taxi drivers were remarkably good even if the passengers had only a smattering of the language. Where else in the world would you find a fresh flower in a vase fixture in the cab, sometimes complimented by white lace antimacassars over the passenger seat head rests? All this for a few yen flag fall. There were, however, a few taxi drivers who were quite reckless. They were known as the Toyoto Crown kamikaze. There was a jingle to the opening tune of the show Oklahoma which went something like this "Yokohama where the kamikaze taxi drivers go..."

For a time I was assigned to the job of being in charge of the bank's telegrams department. A secure telex machine had recently been installed to transmit and receive all our telegraphic communications. Most of the telex traffic was in authenticated plain language but deciphering coded messages could be quite demanding especially if the required code books were not the Bank's own. I was required to be in the office before 7.30am 7/7 in time to telephone the manager Verne Parker having breakfast at home. I had to inform him of the Reuters closing foreign exchange rates in London and New York and anything else of importance particularly messages from Head Office. I had other duties known in the bank such as "opinions" and bank agency arrangements. Opinions stood for the compilation of reports concerning the credit worthiness of trading companies in response to overseas trade enquiries. Invaluable in this work was the Japanese adviser Haiashi san. He was a retired Bank of Tokyo official who had much folk knowledge of Japanese business. Put simply, bank agency arrangements were controlled by Head Office who advised branches to update changes from time to time. In the late 1950's Japan was just beginning to boom after the ravages of war. Inflation was rising rapidly eroding the purchasing power of salaries.

The bank introduced a basket of groceries concept designed to keep salaries universally as level as possible. I recall being offered a placement of an issue of shares in a company called SONY. Much to my ongoing regret I had no spare cash to invest at the time. As the telegrams officer I was expected to be in the office early. Accordingly, I was provided with a small Japanese style house in Kojimachi near the British Embassy and within walking distance of the office. On Sunday mornings after my work in the office I would often go next door to the Foreign Correspondents Club where they served a brilliant brunch with great bloody marys. Most days I enjoyed the walk halfway round the imperial moat to the office in Naka 9 building in Chiyoda ku. Other tenants in the building were Swires and Lowe Bingham Lackie the accountants. Years later I was very pleased to see Willem Mullock Houwer and his delightful wife Lindi at Willem's 70th birthday celebrations in Provence South of France. I was also delighted to have a catchup dinner with Kai Falkman in Stockholm after a 50 year gap. Kai had become a retired ambassador with a charming wife and had written a book in the Haiku discipline.

I was sorry to leave Tokyo on transfer to the bank's Osaka office.

It was not until 1975 that I returned briefly to Tokyo as a guest of Mitsui & Co at the Okura hotel. Mitsui shipbuilding were building a tanker for my friend Nick Embiricos's family. At the very kind invitation of Nick and his wife Valda my wife Lesley and I were part of the "Sivana" launching party which took place in the inland sea.

Geisha party given by Mitsui &Co.

). 1016 M.T. "SIVANA" 16TH JUNE, 1975 LAUNCHING

Ship launching presentations to Nick and Valda.

On the subject of ships it was occasionally my turn to relieve Ivan
Wheeler the Yokohama office manager so that he could play weekend
golf. It usually meant being in charge of the office Friday and Saturday
morning. We in the bank had a saying "any fool can get through a
Saturday morning". One weekend on my watch a very agitated John
Coatsworth the Cunard agent in Japan arrived in the Yokohama office
to say the Queen Mary had been impounded by the Japanese Maritime
Services. It transpired that on leaving Yokohama harbour the ship had
struck the breakwater. Although the ship remained seaworthy there was
damage to the breakwater stonework.

The Japanese decided to impound the ship until a surety was
received guaranteeing to meet the cost of making good the damaged
breakwater. Not least on account of the demurrage this event triggered a
frenetic exchange of telegrams between us and Barclays Bank, Cunard's

bankers in Liverpool. Once we were satisfied Barclays had provided us with the required guarantee through HSBC London, I was able to give Coatsworth the counter guarantee the Japanese required from us. Alas Coatsworth returned to the bank to say the Japanese had changed their mind and wanted ¥2 million in cash. After yet another flurry of telegrams we agreed to provide the cash. The problem was, we didn't have it. Eventually we were able to arrange for a cash delivery from The Bank of Tokyo. The cash was counted in the presence of Coatsworth who took it away in a large suitcase only to return to say the Maritime Services Agency did not want to keep the cash over the weekend because they didn't have a secure safe. I had to point out to Coatsworth that as it was after banking hours on Saturday, I could not give Cunard credit for the cash over the weekend. It was agreed to seal the suitcase and keep it in the bank's vault until Monday. Finally on Monday, the suit case was collected, cash was paid and the ship released. Thus ended what was supposed to be, for me, a quiet uneventful weekend!

The Kansai

The Kansai is the industrial heart of Japan the main cities being Osaka and Kobe.

On my transfer to Osaka office I took the bullet train and much enjoyed a variety of bento boxes offered at station platforms en route.

Unlike high street retail banks in Japan, HSBC did not have much of a deposit base. Liquidity constraints meant our term lending capacity was limited.

Our core business was therefore short term foreign trade finance. Often, reciprocity permitting, we could restrict negotiations under our import l/c's to our own overseas offices thus profiting from both sides of the book. The business could even be self financing by discounting derivative bank accepted term bills of exchange in the money market.

As the New York Jewish bordello mama San said "What a wonderful business, you got it, you sell it, you still have it!"

I was given accommodation in the Kobe HSBC bachelors mess, a rambling bungalow of no architectural merit.

Apart from the HSBC juniors there were two paying guests, Alva. A young Swede who worked for SKF and Mike Farley a junior shipping agent with McKinnon Mackenzie the P&O agents. There were very few public holidays in Japan. I recall feeling particularly deprived trudging through the snow in Osaka on my way to the office on Christmas day. Including the commuting time from Kobe we often worked about twelve hours weekdays and longer on balance nights. We had Saturday afternoons free. Tony Rainer and Fran his attractive American wife lived in a small house near the mess. Tony worked for Swires and boasted he had once not taken leave for 12 years. Years later I saw Tony in Hong Kong wearing his brigade tie as usual and enjoying running the travel agency business of Swires.

Earthquake tremors were not uncommon in Kobe. We probably experienced about a dozen or so a year but thankfully registering only 2 or 3 on the Richter scale.

After the sardine like standing only commuting between Yokohama and Tokyo it was rare not to have a seat on the frequent trains between Kobe and Osaka. I decided against buying a car in favour of hiring one when needed.

The Bank had a presence in Japan since the Meiji period in the 1860's. Then as now the main business was, inter-alia, the finance of foreign trade and it's derivatives. Osaka was a very busy office handling a large volume of import and export letters of credit. We dealt in documents not goods. I recall on the export side one amazing item was chocolate covered ants.

I had a hand in drafting an unusually complex import irrevocable documentary letter of credit covering the construction and delivery of a large floating dock from Holland to Japan. Progressive payments were allowed against documents evidencing completed building stages. Thereafter payments were allowed at each port the towed floating dock passed en route to Japan. The dock was too big to pass through the Suez Canal and had to be towed round the Cape. There was a final turnkey payment when the floating dock was in place and handed over to the owners. The whole operation took almost a year.

Robbie Robertson, a Scot, was the manager of Osaka the accountant being Martin Curran. In due course Martin was to enjoy a meteoric promotion to Deputy Chairman in Hong Kong. As head of Books in Hong Kong I had to work closely with him in calculating the Bank's consolidated annual profit in the colony. After many late hours the profit and loss figures were spread out on a schedule. Martin and I would take the schedule to Jake Saunders the chairman. Sir John who was not known for his wizardry with figures took one look at the schedule (showing the bank's profit for the year) and boomed "what the hell is all this?" With typical thoroughness the Chairman was soon looking into every detail of the results which some would describe as an "embarrassment des riches" whereas we in the bank would have said "quite satisfactory".

Reverting to Robbie Robertson in Osaka. A "Captain Mannering "type" he was popular with the Scottish community., A few weeks before St. Andrew's day he would allow Scottish country dancing practice to take place in the Osaka office banking hall after banking hours. Occasionally the dancing practices would clash with a bank balance night. Balancing the current account ledgers with the journals was a weekly event and meant working late. There was nothing more disconcerting than trying to concentrate against the hoots and yells of the dancers to the gramophone sound of "Jimmy Shand" and wee Robbie striding around the banking hall in a kilt playing the bagpipes. Och Aye!

Eventually my four year tour of Japan came to an end. After dashing through the rain on the tarmac at Tokyo airport I boarded the 'plane in first class to be immediately offered a cigarette and a martini before take off for Copenhagen via Alaska, on the new SAS route over the North Pole.

CHAPTER TEN

London/India

In 1961, having completed a four year tour in Japan, I relished the thought of eight months leave.

At the start of my leave I flew from Tokyo to Madrid. In Madrid I stayed at The Ritz hotel for two nights. In those days, after Spain's isolation under Franco, The Ritz was run down, musty, and badly in need of upgrading. I spent the time mostly shopping for antiques and sampled many sherries from the antique dealers. I also enjoyed tapas bars, and an all too brief visit to The Prado. Leaving Madrid I picked up a P&O ship at Gibraltar and disembarked in Blighty at Southampton. Almost immediately, I had to go down to Antibes in the South of France at the invitation of my parents who had rented a villa there. My sister and brother in law Bruce Clark and their children were also there. Most days I would take the children, Angela and Nicholas, to La Garoupe the nearby beach. By coincidence my friend Gawaine Baillie was competing in a car rally and was staying at the Negresco hotel in Nice. Monsieur Delacroix the Jaguar agent for France gave a splendid dinner for the racing drivers and, being a friend of Gawaine, he very kindly included me. After the dinner Gawaine and I sampled the limited night life of the Riviera.

On my return to London I was delighted to receive a letter from HSBC London office advising me that at the expiration of my leave, my next destination was to be Hong Kong. I was told I was to become head of the current accounts department in Hong Kong office. The department was one of the biggest of it's kind in the world and I was looking forward to the assignment hugely.

Model Helen sues banker

Express Staff Reporter

HELEN CURTIS, 26-year-old London model, has filed a High Court writ claiming damages for alleged breach of promise against 36-year-old merchant banker Alexander Ferguson McCardle, of Culross-street, Mayfair.

In her writ, Miss Curtis, who lives in Bayswater, claims damages for alleged injury to her feelings and loss of prospects of marriage.

Mr. McCardle, who works for a banking firm with offices in the Far East, said last night: "This is very distressing and I shall defend the case."

Author in London 1961

Courtesy of Daily Express/N&S Syndication

My friend Michael Selway had inherited a splendid house in Culross Street Mayfair. It was next door to Angus Ogilvy, who was courting Princess Alexandra at the time. During my leave I was given the use of the house except for one room being used by Michael as an office. So in these splendid surroundings all I had to do was furnish the place with a girl friend. I renewed my relationship with Helen, a girl friend of four years ago. Helen went away for a spell on a modelling assignment. After a time, as fate would have it, I met and fell in love with Wendy Power a debutante. I had known Wendy's sister Judy some years before she married Shaun Plunket.

Unfortunately on Helen's return she overheard an intimate telephone conversation I was having with Wendy. There followed a very acrimonious break up between us, culminating in Helen, understandably, storming out of the house in a fury. She was persuaded by a solicitor friend to sue me for breach of promise, even though we were never engaged. The case was soon dropped, but not before it was front page news in some newspapers. There is nothing I hate more than to cause emotional distress to anyone, let alone someone once dear. However, in life, I'm afraid the power of love can be irresistible, especially at a time of tangled emotions. Following the newspaper reports, and my engagement to Wendy, I received a call from HSBC London office to say that Head Office were taking a dim view of my being featured in the newspapers. The case was dropped, but the unwelcome publicity resulted in my posting being changed from Hong Kong to India. Understandably, the Bank Chairman, Jake Saunders, did not want to risk the Hong Kong newspapers picking up on the story, and felt that I should be "buried" in India for a spell.

I decided to proceed to India by ship. My "Passage to India" was by P&O liner Southampton to Bombay. On disembarkation, I flew to Calcutta where I was accommodated in Goody and Bicky Oberoi's

Great Eastern Hotel in Park Street, The Oberoi's were indefatigable entertainers who, because they were good foreign exchange earners, could be relied upon to offer French champagne, even in austerity India.

The bank was situated in Dalhousie Square not far from the site of the infamous black hole of Calcutta. I was assigned the job of taking over from Indian Officers so that they could take leave. The job meant that I had to take over every department for short periods in both Calcutta and Bombay offices. My first day in Calcutta office the burra babu (head clerk) Hamanta Bose announced a "Pens down" strike for two hours in support of higher pay. Not very long after that it was discovered that the filing clerk, who literally lived in the bank's underground vault, had contracted leprosy. This meant all of us had to wear white cotton gloves to avoid contact with papers he might have handled. At that time India was very short of foreign exchange and imports were drastically curtailed. On taking over the inward bills department I found a significant part of the business was processing barter documents from The State Bank of the U.S.S.R. covering the import of used Russian machinery, in exchange for shipments of cashew nuts. The machinery was often rusted beyond use, whereas the Russians were selling the cashew nut barter shipments for dollars in Hamburg. On a visit to Delhi for a meeting with the Governor of the Reserve Bank of India, I accompanied Joe Lever, the Burra Sahib or senior HSBC manager in India. Amongst other things Joe Lever explained to the Governor our reservations about barter trade with Russia. It seemed to us India should sell it's export produce for dollars, and buy NEW machinery with the proceeds. Perhaps there were other considerations for keeping the barter trade going, as nothing seemed to change. After the visit to Delhi it was arranged that I should visit a customer near Benares. The customer was a company owned by an English family in the business of manufacturing and exporting hand woven carpets.

The bank had extended to them a long standing, well conducted, line of credit against export Letters of Credit and other collateral. Head Office advised that, according to their records, no one had visited the customer for many years. Having been handed the job, I managed to make my way through the bedlam of Howra railway station and eventually found my sleeping compartment in the overnight train to Benares. In the compartment was a large empty ice, box I was able to fill the box by purchasing block ice for a few rupees from the ice wallahs (sellers) on the platform. The conductor woke me in good time to prepare to disembark at a whistle stop station, in the middle of nowhere, some distance before Benares. There was no one in attendance at the station and worse, no one to meet me. The intense heat seemed to engender an oppressive silence interspersed with the shrill chorus of cicadas. After what seemed an age, my customer, in the shape of a very pleasant young Englishman, full of apologies, arrived in a battered Land Rover. On arriving at the business premises, I was surprised to find that, apart from two large storage sheds, there was no factory! It was explained that the "factory" was really a cottage industry. The modus operandi of producing the carpets meant that the weavers were given carefully weighed materials. From these the carpets were made in the weaver's cottages. The finished carpets were then brought back for weighing and, accordingly, the weaver was paid. The finished carpets would go into storage until there was sufficient to fill an export order. Being a good foreign exchange earner, the industry was encouraged by the Government. I much enjoyed meeting the young English family who owned the business. They invited me to lunch in their bungalow. During the lunch I was startled when the gardener came into the dining room with a large dead snake on a stick. This was his way of justifying his keep. Having just got over the shock of the first snake, the gardener appeared 20 minutes later with another one! Before leaving, I was shown an old sailing ship mast. The story was that the mast had been brought up from Calcutta many years ago to be used as a loom component in the manufacture of the biggest one piece carpet ever made in India. The carpet was custom made to fit a huge room in a government building in Delhi.

Actor On stage. Bombay Amateur Theatricals 1963.

The return journey was uneventful, and I was able to report that all seemed well with our customer's carpet business, and, of course, our position as lender.

Morarji Desai the Governor of the state of Maharashtra had introduced prohibition. This meant that Bombay was "dry". On my assignments to Bombay I had to ask the local doctor for a certificate certifying that I was an "alcoholic." Armed with the certificate one was given alcohol coupons. The coupons allowed the holder to buy either a bottle of Indian whisky (Black knight) or six bottles of Indian beer per week. Prohibition meant that social life in Bombay was somewhat subdued, During one of my assignments to Bombay I was persuaded to take the part of David Bullock in an amateur stage production of "The Reluctant Debutante", I enjoyed playing the role hugely and was amazed to receive a good review from the critics. In Bombay I was accommodated in a bank flat on Malabar Hill. The flat had a large balcony and was near a Brahmin burial tower. It was the custom to place dead bodies on a grill on top of the tower so that vultures could eat the flesh. The flesh eaten, the bones would then drop through the grill to be collected at the bottom of the tower. Due to the close proximity of the tower to my balcony, it was disconcerting to sometimes find the odd finger dropped by a vulture!

Inevitably, due to the tyranny of time and distance, my engagement to Wendy came to a poignant end.

No wedding bells for Wendy, the girl who said 'I'll wait'

MISS WENDY POWER (18), who agreed to her mother's suggestion to wait six months before marrying City merchant banker Mr. Alexander McCardle, has called the wedding off.

Miss Power's elder sister Judith recently married Mr. Shaun Plunket at a wedding attended by the Queen Mother.

It was shortly after that that Wendy announced she wanted to marry "Sandy" McCardle, who had received a writ for alleged breach of promise from fashion model Helen Curtis.

"We were meant for each other," said Wendy.

Mr. McCardle was due to return to Hongkong where he had been posted. The wedding was planned for September.

Yesterday Mrs. Power told me: "We hope to issue an official statement soon that the wedding is off. Mr. McCardle? He is somewhere in the West Indies."

WENDY POWER.

The tyranny of distance.

Apart from a painful bout of dengue fever in Kuala Lumpur, I was fortunate to enjoy good health during my Far Eastern tours, until my arrival in India.

Alas, on moving from The Great Eastern Hotel, Calcutta, into a bank owned apartment in Middleton Mansions I came down with dysentery.

I became ill during the night and, in the morning, my bearer found me naked on the bathroom floor in a wretched state. I was carted off to hospital where I found myself in a world of dazzling white mosquito nets under gentle fans, being looked after by gorgeous nurses in immaculate starched uniforms. I made a rapid recovery and was soon back in the office.

Climbing Mt. Everest was never on my bucket list but I could not resist an invitation to fly along the Himalayas and over Mt. Everest. A relative of Dawn, my girl friend at the time, operated a small airfreight service out of Dum Dum airport. He owned and piloted a war surplus twin engined Dakota. It was arranged that he would take Dawn and I on one of his trips.

Baiya Cooch Behar and me in fancy dress Tollygunge Club Calcutta 1963.

We set off from Dum Dum airport at 5am and flew north west towards Kathmandu. On approaching the Himalayas we flew along the Nepal side until we reached Mt. Everest majestically glowing pink in the morning sun. We did two very low passes over the top of Everest allowing us to witness stunning mountain scenery from an unusual angle. We could virtually reach out of the 'plane and scoop up a handful of snow from the peak. My de facto conquest of Everest was an adventure I will never forget. On the return journey we landed at Darjeeling to deliver and pick up freight. During the flight, I was kept busy changing over the wireless transmitters. The stack of fixed frequency wireless transmitters needed changing often, so that we could transmit at different stages of the flight to air traffic controllers.

Social life in Calcutta largely centred around a few clubs. The Bengal Club was the preserve of the Burra Sahibs. We Chotta Sahibs congregated mostly at The Tollygunge Club and the Saturday Club. The poolside crows at The Saturday Club were a nuisance. On more than one accession I have had a sandwich snatched out of my hand by them. My colleague John Gray and I gave a number of cocktail parties at Middleton Mansions and fancy dress balls were great fun at The Tollygunge Club. Firpos and The Blue Fox night club were popular with the late revellers.

John Gray and I would occasionally go shooting. I'm afraid not on exciting tiger hunts but, rather, the more mundane sport of shooting snipe.

The marsh land near Dum Dum was our happy hunting ground. We found the trick in shooting snipe was to stamp on the springy marshy ground and, at the same time, fire about a meter above a rising bird. If you were lucky the snipe would rise into the shot before it could start to zig zag. It was traditional to reward the gun bearers with a gun and one cartridge each at the end of the shoot. The idea was to give them the chance to shoot something for their family pot. I am afraid the gun bearers were not very sporting. They would take the guns and look for flightless paddy birds. Invariably they would stalk the wading birds until they could fire on two together. We always hired the same gun bearers. They were nicknamed Dum and Dumer.

Almost everyone remembers where they were when they heard the news of President Kennedy's assassination. In my case, on November 22nd 1963, I was visiting Bangkok, and heard the news on a taxi wireless in Wireless Road.

In due course, my three year tour of India came to an end and it was time to move on.

CHAPTER ELEVEN

Fully Stretched

On completion of my three year tour of India, I was looking forward to six months leave. At the start of my leave, I flew from Calcutta to Zurich. The shock of clean, prosperous Switzerland, after the deprivations of austerity India took a bit of absorbing. I stayed in a hotel in Zurich for two days. Having slept in the luxury of gleaming white starched sheets, breakfast was a huge treat. I had not seen white sugar, fresh milk and really good bacon and eggs, for years!

On arrival in the UK I spent some time with my family before taking an apartment in London. The apartment was in Princes Court in Brompton Road just across from Harrods. At the time, gambling laws were being relaxed in England and I was introduced to some of the new clubs and casinos by my friend Frank Plugge. The Knightsbridge Sporting Club was a favourite. The drinks and all night buffet costing a nominal £1, were too good to miss even if one suffered a modest loss at the tables. I followed my own rule of stoping if I won or lost £100. I was never addicted to gambling, an occasional flutter was quite enough for me. The London gaming clubs could not be more different from the Portuguese Macao gambling dens I had visited in the mid 1950's. In Macao there were always frenetic crowds jostling around a smoke filled fetid gallery from which fan-tan betting slips and winnings would go up and down in baskets on pulleys. Sometimes there was a blatant sex show going on nearby.

My great friend Nick Embiricos had become engaged to Valda Rogerson. Valda was not only a great beauty but was also a very accomplished point to point rider having won many races.

To celebrate his engagement, Nick gave, what was, one of the best parties I can remember. The event had an Arabian theme with almost everyone in Arab dress. There were even camels wondering around between bonfires, and there was dancing until the wee hours.

I was advised by HSBC London office that my next destination, at the end of my leave, was to be Hong Kong. I was to take over the job of Head of books department. The department was responsible, inter alia, for keeping the consolidated general ledger of all the Bank's operations in Hong Kong. To me this was a huge challenge, and I was looking forward to the assignment.

Book office triumvirate. Self, Mike Uttley,,and ChrisChub at my wedding reception Peninsula Hotel Kowloon 1967

My leave came to an end and I flew to Hong Kong. Skirting the Chinese washing poles the 'plane landed at Kai Tak airport, where I was met by one of the bank's local staff. I was allocated a very spacious and comfortable bank owned apartment in the mid levels. The apartment was staffed by a nice Chinese live-in couple. The husband acted as cook//butler or "boy", while his wife, the Amah, looked after cleaning and laundry. They both wore a uniform of black samfoo trousers and a white tunic with polished brass buttons. The wife had a traditional queue (pigtail). Both had been in the Bank's service for many years, and were obviously pleased to be looking after a bachelor rather than a family with young children. It was about this time that traditional Chinese servants were becoming hard to find. Those who might have gone in to domestic service were being lured abroad or into factory work. The gap was being filled by migratory staff from the Philippines.

Lesley and me, Jeremy Macay and friend aboard the the m.v. Wayfoong.

Just before my arrival in Hong Kong, my Scottish friend Harry Lee, from whom I was to takeover Books department, was drowned. He was trying to save his young son being swept out to sea. The son was saved, but sadly Harry perished. This tragedy meant that, apart from losing a dear friend, I would not have the benefit of a proper handover. A stand in had been coopted to run the department until my arrival. I took over, but it was clear the department was in some need of reorganisation. My responsibilities included, maintaining the bank's consolidated general ledger for Hong Kong, setting foreign exchange rates, note issue transactions, consolidating Colony profit and loss results, and more, much more! The Hang Seng Bank and The Far East Bank, having had liquidity difficulties, were under the aegis of HSBC. In other words the day to day accounting of all HSBC transactions in Hong Kong. Like any other business the bank had to keep books. Prior to computerisation the sheer volume of paper work alone kept the department fully stretched. Just to keep pace with the work I found myself working from 7am straight through often to 2am the next morning most week days. This went on for about eighteen months. I enjoyed some time off on Saturdays, getting away about 4pm. I seemed to manage the very long hours on a diet of black coffee and cigarettes. It was necessary t o work for a few hours on Sunday mornings. Accounting for the sheer volume and complexity of Hong Kong office related foreign exchange transactions occurring all over the world was, in itself, extremely demanding. When I took over the department, it was discovered that there was a huge number of unresponded items in respect of inter branch accounts, notably London and New York. The number of items to be reconciled was about three meters of adding machine print out. With the help of the deputy chairman Freddy Knightly, a team of hand picked senior experienced clerks were allocated a room in which to reconcile all the unresponded items. One item of serious concern was a large payment made by the bank in Hong Kong on the instructions of an Indonesian Bank. In accordance with Agency arrangements the sterling equivalent should have been paid into our account with London office, but wasn't. Through our Djakarta office we were able to recover the money. The clerks in their secluded room did excellent work, and in due course all the un responded items were reconciled except those quantifying to a few HK dollars. It would have been counter productive to continue to pay the cost of staff to look for this trivial amount, and so it was reluctantly written off.

A colleague was put in charge of computerisation. I had to see him in his office concerning fixing a US$ exchange contract to pay for the IBM computer on order. He was so stressed he opened his attaché case and, to my astonishment, produced a meat cleaver, and said "anyone who upsets me to-day, gets this!" This is an illustration of what stress can do.

The biggest cyclical expansion of the note issue occurred just before Chinese New Year. Notes in circulation had to be increased to meet the Chinese custom of settling outstanding debts in cash, before the end of their year. I had to instruct London office to pay the Bank of England the sterling equivalent for every HK$ increase in the note issue. The Bank of England on receipt of the funds would advise The Hong Kong Treasury to issue the required amount of notes. The store of un issued notes were kept in a joint combination walk in safe in the Bank. A treasury official had one combination and the Bank had the other. Under our joint supervision the notes were counted out and taken upstairs to the bank's cash department for distribution. After Chinese New Year the reverse procedure was followed. The Hong Kong Treasury would instruct The Bank of England to Pay our London office the sterling value of the notes taken out of circulation. Jake Saunders, the Chairman, felt it was unreasonable for the Bank of England to deduct one eighth of a penny in the case of a contraction in the note issue. In other words we lost one eighth of a penny several million times depending on the value of the note issue contraction. I was asked to appeal to The Hong Kong Treasury to waive the deduction pointing out that HSBC not only paid Waterlow or De La Rue to print the notes, but we also paid for freight, insurance, engravers art work, storage, and the cost of additional shroffs (cashiers) to handle large note issues and contractions, not to mention some loss of earnings on the counterpart funds paid to the Bank of England. The Hong Kong Treasury listened, but were unwilling to give up this contentious item of revenue. They argued that they too had costs and that we should regard the levy as an advertising expense. They said that with the privilege of the bank's name on the notes, what better advertising could we have? It was difficult to argue with that. The Hong Kong Government's laissez-faire policy, and low corporate tax on a highly profitable business, enabled the bank to advantageously build up an enviable cash chest with which to make future acquisitions and expand profitably.

The end of the financial year was an extremely busy time for Book office.

Consolidating the colony's P&L results was a complex and difficult task, not made any easier by some branches changing their figures. The manager of Mongkok office and I had words when he amended his figures not once, but three times.

Foreign exchange was a substantial profit earner for the Bank. In book office, one of my duties was to set the exchange rates each day, for certain currencies. This had to be done early in the morning well before the banks in Hong Kong opened for business.

Using the Reuters closing currency exchange rates in London and New York the rates would be calculated on a loaded formula agreed between HSBC, and our main competitor The Chartered Bank.

A printout of the new exchange rates would be circulated daily to departments and branches in the colony. Banks were free to quote what they liked on minor currencies. We had to deal with incessant telephone calls from branches seeking guidance and rates in order to fix forward exchange contracts for customers. We had an efficient reporting system in place so that at close of business each day we could readily see which currencies were overbought or oversold. I was then able to telegraphically instruct overseas branches and correspondents to buy or sell currencies as appropriate to square our position. In that way, at least theoretically, our exchange risk was extinguished. In fact, because of time differences, it was conceivable that markets could change before our instructions could be implemented. This meant that, until our instructions were actually carried out, we, unavoidably, carried an overnight exchange risk. We routinely had to fund our overseas accounts to meet commercial Letter of Credit drawings and other contingencies. This often meant using a range of currency dealing options. In considering the various options available, the focus was always on what would be the most profitable outcome. We were not in the business of taking exchange risks. Avoiding exchange risk and keeping a safe margin of liquidity, were always paramount considerations.

At each year end I had to spend a great deal of time with our auditors Peat Maewick & Michell and Lowe Bingham & Matthews. Amongst other things, they wanted to know everything about each and every general ledger account. Entries relating to our relationship with the The Far East Bank and the Hang Seng Bank also had to be explained. It was interesting to see the auditor's eyes glazing over when I attempted to explain the mysteries of the "Gold Account" to them.

Phillip Stubbs held the Godlike position of Manager Hong Kong. He was a very able charismatic banker who's father had been a previous Governor of Hong Kong. He would often summon departmental heads to his office at short notice. He seemed, however, to have a more deferential approach to book office. To his credit, he would telephone and ask if it was convenient for him to come to see me! A gesture I much appreciated in a strict culture of vertical management.

Some bonuses were paid to senior management. The amounts were quite modest and would be considered derisory in to-day's world. In those days, even if you were making very substantial attributable profits for the Bank, it was considered that "you were just doing your job." At the time the Chairman's emoluments included a bonus equal to a percentage of the bank's annual profit. From his bonus the chairman would disburse bonus payments of varying amounts to his senior managers and some other staff.

The bonus payments were highly confidential and it was my job to keep a handwritten ledger of the bonus accounts in my office safe. For those who did not receive a bonus, there was a joke doing the rounds; Q. What are the three most useless things in the world?

A. The Pope's balls, a man's tits, and a vote of thanks to the staff!

Nowadays, contractual profit related bonuses are often subject to restrictive drawdown and claw back clauses. Critics of large, and very large bonuses, often forget that the amounts usually represent only a tiny percentage of the profit earned for the Bank by the bonus recipient. Those who preach for a "fairer society would do well to recognise the huge taxes levied on bank profits, and on banker's emoluments. It is said the definition of a communist is, "One who wants an equal share of other people's earnings!"

After a hectic two years, my stint in book office came to an end.

I was unexpectedly appointed to take over from the sub accountant who was going on short leave. The job was more to do with administration rather than banking. It was known as the job nobody wanted. I was fortunate to have the benefit of a well experienced staff to assist in managing the hundreds of local staff, and the management and maintenance of the bank's extensive properties. The bank employed a cadre of staff of mixed Portuguese descent. They generally worked in different areas from the Chinese staff. Years before, senior management felt that, for security reasons, the two ethnic groups would "keep an eye on each other". Much time was spent on local staff recruitment, revising wage schedules, leave schedules, and the provision of a range of benefits, including health care, and superannuation. Dismissing staff was a rare occurrence. Occasionally a local staff funeral had to be arranged! A new professional property department was being formed to maintain and manage the bank's extensive commercial and residential properties. Even so, I still had to deal with some minor aspects of preliminary planning for the new Foster's bank building in prospect.

After three months the sub accountant returned from leave and I was able to hand the department back to him. To me, my time in book office and my short stint in running the sub accountants department were testing experiences I would not have wished to miss.

After handing the department back to the sub accountant, I was immediately appointed to Head Office staff as an assistant branch controller, or "ticker". All I had to do was clear my desk and move upstairs to "the corridors of power."

CHAPTER TWELVE

Head Office and Marriage

The first thing that struck me on arrival in Head Office, was the silence.

I was allotted a desk in a large room with five other assistant branch controllers. No one spoke in the library like atmosphere, the silence being punctuated by the odd cough, or the snap of a cigarette lighter. Up till then I had always been used to working amid the "buzz" of busy departments.

Head Office exercised tight control over overseas operations. I was allocated Singapore, Malaysia, Thailand, and Indonesia. To enable us to monitor operations, branches were required to submit comprehensive monthly returns. Analysing these returns on a month on month basis gave one a surprisingly good understanding of branch operations. Some useful statistics were obtained by extracting data from the returns. For ease of administration, correspondence with branches was mostly conducted on a semi official basis. Occasionally branches might disagree with HO. The last word was, of course, always with the controller overseas operations.

So as not to discourage managers in the field, Head Office liked to portray an image of paternalistic guidance. Internecine managerial disagreements were very rare.

One of my jobs was to assist with proof reading the annual report to shareholders. To me, this tedious task was reminiscent of Oscar Wilde spending an entire morning trying to decide if he should take out a comma from something he had written. He did, only to spend the whole back breaking afternoon deciding to put it back again! After the annual general meeting it was customary for the Directors to send up a few bottles of their champagne to Head Office. I, for one, was very pleased to enjoy the novelty of some Pol Roger at my desk, even if it was from a paper cup!

Dick Lloyd was the very capable keeper of Head Office Books. he was responsible for keeping the accounts of the entire bank. Occasionally I was detailed to assist him in his work, especially if protocol demanded a four eyes (two people) authorisation, such as an investment transfer from the bank pension fund. In my work I needed access to Head Office archives. There were many confidential files in the archives. Staff files, however, were highly confidential and for the eyes of the Chairman and the Staff Controller only. I was told the Chairman never saw his own staff file. It was the custom for the outgoing Chairman to destroy his successor's file before handing over the job.

At this time my life revolved around work and courting my wife to be.

In 1966 Hong Kong experienced one of the worst tropical storms for many years. On a Sunday morning I awoke, and was thinking about going into the office for an hour or so, I became aware of an unusual roaring noise outside the window. On opening the curtains I could see the cause of the noise was heavy rain of an unbelievable intensity. The rain continued unabated. At midday, just before the telephones went dead, I received a call from a friend advising me not to attempt to use my car and to have a look at Conduit Road. I struggled out in the intense storm and reached Conduit Road at the bottom of the drive. The road had disappeared and in it's place was a surging river, fed by torrents of rainwater cascading down from the Peak. Driverless cars were eerily floating past together with a variety of debris. Clearly I was marooned. Night came with no respite. The rain finally abated early next morning.

Getting to the office on foot was a daunting task. Conduit Road had drained, but there were so many obstacles and piled up cars blocking the road it was impossible to drive. I managed to find a way onto the Peak Tram track and by that route was able to reach Des Voeux Road and the Bank. No traffic was running and parts of the road were ankle deep in water. I will never forget the incongruity of entering the bank in bare feet, with my trousers rolled up and my shoes tied around my neck. Land slides had occurred causing a large apartment tower to collapse with considerable loss of life. Only a few of us managed to reach Hong Kong office. A helicopter was organised to drop a walkie talkie telephone to the Chairman marooned in his house on the Peak. The next day the Chairman, Jake Saunders, was airlifted down from the Peak by helicopter. The bank was soon functioning with a skeleton staff, and as soon as public transport was restored we were able to operate normally. With typical thoroughness the Hong Kong authorities organised a massive cleanup operation and within a week or so the colony was almost back to normal.

The floods were in sharp contrast to water rationing in the long hot riot torn summer of 1967. The catchments on the island were nearly dry and there were difficulties in obtaining adequate water piped from the mainland. As a result, water rationing was put in place. My allowance was 4 inches of bath water per week. The ration was meant to cover everything, including cooking, washing, and loo flushing. Hotels were exempt from water rationing, so in desperation, for a time, a few of us clubbed together to take a room in the Mandarin Hotel just to use the shower. Easily the most expensive showers I have ever had, but worth it in the heat and humidity of mid summer Hong Kong. Looking back courting my wife to be was difficult, as we were separated by the harbour. Due to my working hours, seeing my fiancée often meant dodging curfew restrictions. After the last ferry, I was obliged to keep the cross harbour walla wallas (small ferry boats) busy.

I met Lesley, my wife to be, at a dinner party given by Mok Ying Kee a leading Hong Kong stockbroker. I felt fortunate to be seated beside a gorgeous Australian girl who turned out to be Lesley. Before long we became an "item", enjoying life hugely as lovers do. Lesley's arrival in Hong Kong was a long journey, beginning when she graduated in pharmacy from Sydney university before taking a year off to travel in Europe. She was sailing with Paul Ritchie, amongst others, on Fulke Warwick's yacht in the Mediterranean. On the yacht she was told that her parents had been run down by a car in Sydney. Her mother was badly injured, and her father was killed. Her father, Bill Gerrett, was a well known chartered accountant and company director in Sydney. She spent the next year looking after her mother in Sydney before setting off for Europe once again. Taking a ship to Singapore, she disembarked and preceded overland through Malaysia, Cambodia and Vietnam. In Vietnam she was just one step ahead of the Viet Cong. Arriving in Hong Kong she was offered the job of pharmacist in the Peninsula Hotel pharmacy. She was well paid and was also given a share of the pharmacy profits. At the same time Peter Gauchy, the Peninsula Hotel General Manager offered her the drinks and beverage franchise of the new prestigious Felix bar and restaurant in the Peninsula annex. She had to purchase all drinks at a fixed price from the Peninsula Hotel and was allowed to charge customers whatever she liked. After paying her staff of three barman and a sommelier, her profit margin was huge. So in effect she was giving customers hangovers in the evening and medicines (if not cures) the next morning in the pharmacy!

A highlight of our courtship was my turn to have the use of the bank's motor vessel The Wayfoong. The boat had been brought down from Shanghai for the recreational use of the Hong Kong foreign staff on a roster basis. If it was my turn, my servants would come on board with pre cooked curry and lots of booze. The captain and crew would be told to proceed and off we would go to some secluded beach, or just weigh anchor somewhere. Lesley was a fearless swimmer and would swim off the boat almost out of sight. I'm afraid I wasn't so adventurous because of my fear of sharks.

Lesley and I were married in St. Andrews church Kowloon. Neither of our widowed mothers could attend because of ill health. We had our reception sat the Peninsula Hotel and spent the first night of our honeymoon in the very grand Peninsula presidential suite. Next day we flew to Taiwan for our honeymoon at the new Madam Chiang Kai Shek hotel. Unfortunately the hotel was not quite finished and we had to, initially, make do with an uncarpeted bedroom with two small single beds! The museum in Taiwan was a huge treat. We took drives into the country side where we were amazed to find endless fields of pineapple, and bridges built out of locally quarried marble. We enjoyed some really good Chinese restaurants and bought some art. Arriving back in Hong Kong we had two days before flying to Bangkok to take up my next appointment with the Bank.

Wedding reception at Peninsula Hotel Kowloon 1967.

In Hong Kong in 1966 I received the devastating news that my father had died of a heart attack aged 68. His death triggered a family crisis. I inherited some minor debts and the responsibility of looking after my mother who was left unprovided for. I'm sure the maxim "A shroud has no pockets," is more appreciated by those blessed with inheritance. After serving in France during WW1 my father became an entrepreneur. In partnership with his brother, they founded a motor engineering business. After that he was a hotel proprietor, and at one time was the owner of a cinema in the days before mass TV. He died in a rented house having exhausted his savings. At the same time, my brother in law found himself in financial difficulties. His wife, my darling sister, contracted multiple sclerosis and was confined to a wheel chair. My brother in law had to give up his hotel in a country town and embarked on a London pub venture which failed, despite some loans from me. In these circumstances, I had to step in and buy a house big enough to accommodate everyone. In his younger days my brother in law had been the principal bass singer in the Carl Rosa Opera Company. I had seen him perform in the Edinburgh Festival and at Glyndebourne. He had a commanding stage presence and a good voice but, I'm afraid, he did not have much of a head for business. To his credit, after installing his family in the house I provided, he sold his car, bought a bicycle, and devoted his time to looking after his invalid wife and two young children. In due course he was able to move his family to their own house. My mother found a nice couple for the basement flat of my house. The couple, Tom and Ivy, and their budgerigar, had the basement flat rent free in return for the wife looking after my mother and, when needed, acting as a sort of de facto "femme de ménage.»

Parents wedding 1926

CHAPTER THIRTEEN

Bangkok

After the heat, civil unrest, and water shortage of Hong Kong, Bangkok was a quiet, peaceful haven. We took over the well run accountant's house from David and Rena Jaques. The house was one of several in a compound owned by the bank for many years. Each house was discretely hidden from it's neighbour in landscaped grounds of about 3 acres, with a klong (river) running through it. We were well looked after by Ood the housekeeper who was ably assisted by the cook, two cleaners, and a wash amah. One of the cleaners took to wearing my discarded underpants as a dust cap. It was quite disconcerting to see her running around unwittingly advertising "jockey"! There was Sante the driver of the bank car, allotted for my use. Also included in the retinue were about four communal gardeners, a night watchman, and two night sentries guarding the entrance gate to the compound. Looking back, I feel privileged to have experienced what was sadly the end of an era of grand colonial residences and numerous servants. The rising value of land in central Bangkok inevitably meant that the compound had to be sold in keeping with the values of a changing world. The bank had a holiday bungalow on the beach in the quiet fishing village of Pattaya. If it was our turn, we would take a servant and drive down to the bungalow for a relaxing weekend by the sea. At that time there were very few tourists. Keith Hyland was our Australian neighbour in Pattaya. He was in the business of processing, and selling duck feathers collected from all over Thailand and Vietnam. Unfortunately, on a visit to Vietnam he was captured by the Vietcong and held prisoner for some time. A great treat in Pattaya was the periodic visit from the black market man. He would offer scotch whisky and cigarettes at bargain prices. We suspected his source of supply was the nearby American Forces PX. From the same source we were occasionally offered fresh USA milk and T bone steaks. The disappearance of Jim Thompson from a HSBC holiday bungalow in the Cameron Highlands, Malaysia, was a great shock to all who knew him in Bangkok. He was best known for revitalising the Thai silk industry. There were rumours that he was also involved with the CIA. It seems he left the bungalow one evening to go for a walk, and was never seen again.

HSBC Bangkok office staff 1967

Lesley's mother flew up from Sydney for a visit to meet me. She was intelligent and well travelled. I always found her stimulating company, and we became good friends. She was a formidable scrabble player and it was rare for me to win. Nowadays, it is so much easier to play scrabble on an IPad, rather than using a board, tiles, and manual score keeping.

On taking over from David Jaques I was not surprised to find the office in good order. All the revenue departments were operating smoothly and profitably. Sterling devaluation was on the cards, in view of which Head Office exceptionally allowed us to maintain a very modest oversold position in sterling. We subsequently realised a useful exchange gain.

The bachelors mess was situated on the top floor of the bank. Over the years there were numerous stories about the occupants. One such story was about a young bachelor going into his room at Christmas. He found in his bed, a gorgeous young Thai girl with a Christmas card tied to her neck. She was a Christmas present from a customer!

About half way through my Bangkok assignment, I was pleased to welcome John Bond a bright young newly married second tour junior. Before leaving Bangkok I gave him a well deserved good report on his conduct. I was pleased to see, years later, he became HSBC Group Chairman.

After an interesting eight months I handed back the Accountant's role to David Jaques, and proceeded on eight months leave.

CHAPTER FOURTEEN

Baring Bros Goldman Sachs. Morgan Stanley

The second time I had to work in the city was very different to my time as an HSBC Foreign Staff trainee in 1952. Preparatory to opening the Melbourne office of HSBC group in 1968, it was arranged that I should be seconded for short periods to some friendly correspondent financial institutions. Amongst these were Goldman Sachs and Morgan Stanley in New York and Baring Brothers and Smith St Aubyn in London.

I had an introduction to Mr Eggar the head of banking in Baring Brothers. Typical of Baring's rather old fashioned management structure Mr Eggars title was Head Clerk. A very modest title at a time when any junior American banker worth his salt was at least a Vice President. Mr Eggars was a very experienced banker and was good enough to show me something of Baring's banking department operations. In due course I was passed on to Mr Carnwath the Baring's architect of the Save and Prosper managed fund. Perhaps he might have thought me too inquisitive as, very often, tapping his nose, his answer to my questions was "Never let day light on magic!" My secondment to Barings was rounded off spending time in the new issues department. Lord Cromer had just returned to chair Barings after a spell as Governor of The Bank of England. He gave a splendid luncheon in the boardroom to mark his return to the firm. Lord Cromer was good enough to invite me, and I found myself in the company of many city notables. Seated beside the secretary of Lloyds Bank I enjoyed some delicious asparagus brought up from Lord Cromer's estate. Years later I was sorry to hear of the collapse of Baring Bros following the actions of an under supervised rogue trader in Singapore.

Angus McKinnon the chairman of Smith St Aubyn was also chairman of ANZ Bank. I was given some very helpful introductions to people in Melbourne and learned something of the business of Smith St Aubyn in the city. I particularly enjoyed doing the rounds with the bill brokers in their silk hats.

Prior to leaving London I had lunch at The Savoy grill with Sir Alexander Downer the Australian High Commissioner. Sir Alexander was also good enough to give me some useful introductions to Australian contacts.

New York

I arrived in New York from Jamaica in a tropical suit. I stepped off the 'plane into -14 degrees without an overcoat. Having checked into the St Moritz hotel I had to open the window because the bedroom was vastly overheated. I hailed a cab the next morning and asked the driver to take me to Abercrombie and Fitch so that I could buy an overcoat. The driver said I should go to Macy's instead and buy a suit of the newly introduced thermal underwear -- much cheaper. I wanted to try on the underwear at Macy's but was told I could not as it was against health regulations, but a try on would be ok if I bought the underwear. I must admit the thermal underwear was really light and warm and saved me the expense of an overcoat.

At Morgan Stanley I was attached to Dudley Schoals a senior partner in charge of placing government bonds including those of Australia. Dudley's office was filled with his collection of Roman antiquities. We seemed to spend an awful lot of time discussing these. I did, however, learn quite a bit about the placement of government bonds and was given some useful introductions, including Bill McMahon the Australian Treasurer and his charming wife Sonia.

Dudley entertained my wife and I at his splendid house in Westchester County as well as at the Westchester Country Club. He also introduced me to Le Cirque restaurant at the Pierre Hotel and the Oyster Bar at the Plaza. My secondment to Goldman Sachs was an interesting experience. They had rather gloomy offices in which I did my best to learn something of investment banking. In 1967 Goldman Sachs was not then the behemoth it is nowadays. There seemed to be a constant search for investment derivatives for clients. The staff I met were dynamic and helpful.

My wife and I decided to travel to Washington, D.C. by Greyhound bus. It turned out to be not a good idea. We were the only white passengers in a full bus with seats next to the bus lavatory. We enjoyed the sights of Washington and had one of the best Caesar salads I have ever eaten at the Occidental Hotel. The salad was expertly mixed in a large wooden bowl at the table by an engaging coloured waiter who certainly knew what he was doing.

Tourist. With replica of the liberty bell Washington D.C.

I much enjoyed eating out in New York. Generous hosts would take us to such places as, The Pierre Hotel, The Russian Tea Room, the Plaza Oyster Bar, and the Metropolitan Club with it's cavernous dining room. I also very much enjoyed hot pastrami and hamburgers served by numerous delicatessens in Manhattan. Dudley Schoales was kind enough to take me to the New York bankers club from time to time to indulge in his favourite little neck clams.

Given the size of the American national debt, I became aware that there were numbers even larger than a trillion. Take for example the GOOG OL being the figure 1 followed by 100 zeroes Or expressed in another way:

GOOG OL = -10^100

Apart from the ability to accurately add up long columns of figures and interest calculations, I was never very numerate and the appearance of hand held calculators was a godsend to me.

Mobile or cell phones had just made their first appearance. Some were like large bricks whilst others were fitted into attaché cases.

The banking industry was undergoing seismic changes in technology. Computers were rapidly decreasing in size and increasing in use. HSBC in Hong Kong was one of the first banks in the world to go on line using an IBM system. This laudable technological feat was soon complimented by the introduction of the first NCR. Automated Teller Machines in the colony. These machines were a sort of coup de foudre for the bank who quickly stole a march on it's competitors by placing a large maiden order for ATMs on the condition that HSBC would have a monopoly for the machines in Hong Kong for the next three years.

America was a significant contributor in the development of credit cards. In Victorian times it was considered shameful by some to borrow money. Debt was a dreaded word and was to be avoided by most families. This all miraculously changed when bankers decided to semantically change the meaning of the word debt. Why not call it CREDIT instead. So debt became credit and soon everyone was to be issued with a CREDIT card on which they could run up debt. The advent of mass credit card usage was a synergistic bonanza for the banks. Not only could they charge customers for the card but also obtain commission from the vendors, charge high interest rates, gain exchange profit, and benefit from the decrease in the burgeoning cheque clearance burden to name but some of the advantages for the banks. To cap it all, the convenience of credit cards became hugely popular with customers. How could we now manage without them? Nowadays the old perceived stigma of debt has largely disappeared and we even have debit cards.

Whilst in Washington, then as now, on a macro level, people were becoming a bit apprehensive about America's increasing appetite for deficit defence spending and at the same time aspiring to be the world's unilateral policeman. There was also the suspicion that a Government relying on a system of paid lobbying could conceivably create situations of giving power undemocratically to the highest bidder, in other words big business!

I enjoyed my secondments in London and America hugely. The experience was very helpful in preparing me for my assignment in Australia

CHAPTER FIFTEEN

Australia 1967-1973

At the start of leave, we flew from Bangkok to Sydney via Darwin and arrived in Sydney the same day the Australian Prime Minister, Harold Holt, was drowned. Kingsford Smith airport Sydney consisted of two sheds, one for customs and one for passport control and, of course, everyone spoke "strine" (Australian). It reminded me of when I first heard a really strong Australian accent. One evening during the emergency in Malaya I happened to be in The Lucky World in Kuala Lumpur. The Lucky World was a rather sleazy licensed entertainment complex. There was a stage, bars, and a dance hall where taxi dance girls charged 20cents a dance. A group of Australian squaddies (soldiers) came up to me. One of them said "Gidie, looking for the Sheila with the snike", Meaning, "good day, looking for the girl with the snake". They were really looking for Rosie Chan, the entertainer, who was doing a stage act with a boa constrictor. Another "language" story was told to me by my great friend Edward Scott who, after a long spell in Australia, became chairman of Swires. Edward was accompanying a senior Swire director on a visit to Port Moresby, Papua New Guinea. Just before they arrived, the local manager's house boy rushed up to his master to say in pidgeon English "Jesus Christ coming by mix master". He meant that the big boss was arriving by helicopter.

On arrival at the airport we were met by Lesley's sister Pamela and her husband Bryan Young, and their five children. I couldn't have wished for a warmer welcome and was immediately made to feel part of the family. After crowded Hong Kong and Bangkok it was quite strange walking in a Sydney park in the afternoon with no one else in sight.

We spent about two hectic weeks in Sydney with Lesley's family and friends before flying to New York. On leaving New York we took the express lift to the roof of the Pan am building, boarded a helicopter, and we're whisked up the Hudson River to La Guardia airport. Almost immediately we took off, and conveniently landed at Prestwick airport, Scotland.

On holiday in Scotland I received a letter from HSBC London advising me that my destination after leave was to be Australia where I was to open the Melbourne office of the HSBC group. Prior to that, arrangements had been made for me to be assigned, for short periods, to Baring Bros and Smith St. Aubyn in London and, after that, Morgan Stanley and Goldman Sachs in New York.

After leave, I arrived back in Australia and spent some time with Tony Harman the HSBC representative in Sydney before making my way to Melbourne. On arrival in Melbourne I witnessed some lively demonstrations against Australia's involvement in the war in Vietnam. Prime minister Gorton was under pressure to withdraw Australian forces.

First manager HSBC Group in Melbourne 1968.

There were two memorable placards in the Collins Street demonstrations. One proclaimed "If you were being raped, would you demand immediate withdrawal or prolonged negotiations?" The other was simply "Cut off Gorton's penal powers!" On a visit to Australia the Queen was once greeted with a placard in the crowd saying "Gidie Betty, you and Phil on benefits?"

My first priority was to find office premises and accommodation for myself and family. I was able to rent suitable premises in Collins Street opposite to what was then The English Scottish and Australian Bank, ably managed by Max Scambler an astute banker. I was very pleased to be contacted by one of my ex local staff in Books Hong Kong. He and his family had emigrated to Australia and he was looking for a job. I was delighted to take him on together with a secretary, and other staff.

Lesley in Mexico City 1971

Lesley found a suitable apartment to rent in South Yarra. It was the top floor of a Spanish Mission type house fronted by a gated courtyard. We discovered the swimming pool had been filled in and planted with potatoes during the war. We had it excavated just in time for the long very hot summer of 1969.

Not having a banking licence meant that our business was restricted. In time we managed to build up a sizeable money market book. On the asset side lending was for the most part short term property development loans.

I failed to obtain Head Office approval to finance an entrepreneur who had obtained the franchise for Kentucky Fried Chicken outlets. In the event the business proved hugely successful! I had more luck with persuading HO to approve a working capital loan for Rupert Murdoch's business. I negotiated the deal with Mervin Rich, Rupert Murdoch's finance director.

Bryan Young, my brother in law, worked for Rupert Murdoch in Melbourne for a time,

On the TV side Bryan had to host an award event. I was invited and was seated at a table with TV stars and other VIPs. I had the privilege to be seated next to Lady Elisabeth Murdoch who, far sheer charm and intelligence, far outshone anyone else at the table.

One of the highlights of my time in Melbourne was the visit of the HSBC Chairman Jake Saunders. Being a highly decorated war hero Jake was hugely popular with the many veterans in the upper echelons of the Melbourne business and banking fraternity. I hosted a reception for him and surprised myself by remembering the names of over a hundred guests. How I managed that feat of memory I will never know. Having completed three years in Melbourne I was granted six months leave. Lesley wanted to visit Macchu Pichu in Peru whereas I wanted to visit Tahiti, Easter Island and Valparaiso. We decided to go ahead with our respective itineraries and rendezvous in Santiago. I spent two days in Tahiti before flying down to Easter Island. Having read Thor Hyderdahl's "Kon Tiki Expedition" I enjoyed exploring the small island and, in particular, examining the huge stone statues. After a brief look at Valparaiso I touched down in Santiago. I was resting on my bed in my hotel room when I became aware of a strange loud thudding noise on the outside of my bedroom wall behind my head. I looked out of the window to see fighting going on in the streets with bullets flying everywhere. The Allende uprising had began. Midnight came with no sign of Lesley. At about 3am, much to my relief, there was a knock on the door, and there was Lesley. She had been given an army escort from the airport and was utterly exhausted. Her luggage and jewellery had been stolen at the airport. She had empty cigarettes packs in her shoes, the soles of which had worn through. The hotel arranged for an army escort to take us by a circuitous route to the airport where we caught a flight to the peace of Buenos Aires. We enjoyed the restaurants in BA, especially the steaks which somehow were always cooked to perfection. We dropped in to a very respectable night club. The band played only tango and more tango. We went on to Rio de Janeiro from where we caught a flight to Lisbon. After a quick look around Lisbon, we found a nice sea side hotel in Cascais. The hotel served the biggest sardines I have ever seen. The remainder of my leave was spent mostly with family in Scotland.

CHAPTER SIXTEEN

Singapore 1971

I finished my assignment in Melbourne with the satisfaction of having established a sound profitable business for HSBC and with a banking licence in prospect.

My appointment in Singapore was CEO of Malaysian Australian Finance Ltd. MAF was a wholly owned subsidiary of HSBC. Headquartered in Singapore the company also had offices in Malaysia and Brunei. The business was mainly big ticket leasing of high value equipment for the logging industry, helicopter leasing, motor car hire purchase, and vehicle floor plan finance for motor car dealers. The business was highly profitable and was funded in the main by deposits from the public. The hire purchase side of the business was fuelled by the growing appetite for car ownership.

With our new baby Alexandra, we arrived in Singapore and were initially accommodated in the spacious bank flat above the bank's Orchard Road office, which had been bombed by a terrorist during the confrontation with Indonesia.

Mr. Hassan Namazie, of Namazie M. A. (Pte) Ltd.; and Mr. A. F. McCradie, general manager of Malaysian Australian Finance, at Mr. R. B. Moore's farewell party at the Hyatt.

As CEO MAF talking to a Singapore stock broker at HSBC reception.

Alexandra was duly christened at St Andrews cathedral Singapore. Shortly thereafter we moved in to our house in Sri Menanti the bank's gated compound of about 4 acres. The house was about a ten minute drive from the central business district. After DIY Australia we were grateful to have servants again. We employed a cook, housekeeper, cleaner, driver, and an amah for the baby.

There were also communal gardeners and a night watchman. Some years later I was not surprised to hear the value of the compound land had appreciated to the point where, in a changing world, it had to be sold.

I had to visit all of the MAF offices from time to time. Some of the loggers leased equipment of very high value, such as fleets of caterpillar machines. Very occasionally a lessee would fall behind in the agreed monthly leasing payment. To attempt to repossess a huge caterpillar machine out of the jungle was out of the question. Instead, we arranged for one of our repossessors to disable the machine (our machine) at night by removing the distributor. This had the desired effect of persuading the customer to keep his payments up to date. For the most part, we would lease logging equipment only if the customer had an irrevocable letter of credit covering export of the timber harvested. Negotiations under the L/C had to be restricted to HSBC. In that way we were assured of receiving the agreed leasing instalments. Most of the meranti timber was processed into ply wood and shipped to Japan. If there was a downturn in USA house starts demand from Japan would inevitably slow. In these circumstances, we learned that a restricted L/C was of little comfort if the ships were not sent for the timber. In other words, no shipments, no payments. The environmental effect of denuding the jungles of trees is a source of concern to many. Reforestation is desirable, but, sadly, all too often felled trees are never replaced. In global warming discussions, it should never be forgotten that the slightest change in the earth's orbiting tilt could conceivably cause the recurrence of another ice age!

Given the political sensitivity between Malaysia and Singapore the name Malaysian Australian Finance Ltd did not sit well with having our Head Office in Singapore. It was decided to keep the initials MAF and split the company. One half would be incorporated in Singapore and the other incorporated in Kuala Lumpur. The name would be changed to Mortgage and Finance in deference to the established acronym MAF. To keep faith with the new name we allocated a token amount of funds for mortgage lending. In spite of liquidity constraints, no one was clever enough, in those days, to devise a marketable, without recourse, mortgage derivative to facilitate mortgage lending expansion.

I was disappointed to learn that after a short leave I was to relinquish control of the Singapore company and relocate to Kuala Lumpur to resume charge of the Malaysian and Brunei operations.

CHAPTER SEVENTEEN
Rothschild Intercontinental Bank

Whilst on leave in London I received a call, out of the blue, from a firm of management consultants, or head hunters, as they were known as. Out of curiosity I agreed to a meeting with one of the partners. At the meeting it transpired that Rothschild Intercontinental Bank Ltd was looking for an experienced banker to be CEO of their planned operations in Hong Kong. They were offering a most attractive package.

The salary and allowances would be much greater than that of HSBC. Superannuation would be very much better, and instead of mandatory retirement at age 52. I could expect to work until normal retirement at age 65 or longer. It was expected the appointee would initially set up the operation in Hong Kong, before relocating to work in London. I agreed to a series of meetings with Tom Stonor a Director of RIB in London. I enjoyed meeting Tom and was impressed with his enthusiasm and vision. After much in depth discussion, the time came for me to make up my mind about accepting the job offer from RIB.

I agonised for weeks about leaving HSBC. Trying to come to a decision was painful and was certainly a very stressful experience. My leave was coming to an end, and so I could not put off my decision for much longer. Eventually, I decided to accept the offer from RIB and, with the greatest reluctance and regret, resigned from HSBC.

I was not to know then, that I would shortly be embroiled in an internecine power struggle with the paranoid, machiavellian, roguish, N M Rothschild representative in Hong Kong. It would soon become apparent that he saw RIB as a threat to his own position, and was clearly recalcitrant in his willingness to cooperate with me.

Before leaving for Hong Kong, I spent a month or so working in RIB's London office. I met key staff, and studied the workings of most departments. Tom Stonor introduced me to senior management in N M Rothschild Ltd at New Court. I particularly remember my meeting with one of the directors of N M Rothschild. He had just returned from a visit to South America. He showed Tom and I a large diamond ring he had bought in South America. With it, he was hoping to become engaged to Marian Stein. In the event, she married Jeremy Thorpe the leader of the Liberal Party.

I visited Cologne for useful discussions with Bankhaus Sal Oppenheim, an asset management bank and a partner in RIB. I was surprised to see so many women taxi drivers in Cologne. The post war buildings were dismal. On the other hand, I was pleased to see, that somehow, the cathedral had escaped the bombing during the war.

Hong Kong offered a smorgasbord of profitable opportunities for a new bank, and it was my intention to plan an a la carte approach for RIB to follow. Dealing in gold, asset management, money market, corporate advice, where just some of the options to consider. The formation of a strong influential local committee made up of a few highly respected successful local business men, was also something to contemplate. I was constantly turning over in my mind how best to proceed profitably. To my mind, the main problem was finding good executive staff. With the best will in the world I'm afraid I was not always impressed with the banking experience of available RIB staff. Then as now, some of the main ingredients for a successful bank would include, inter alia, sound highly motivated management, risk aversion, adequate capital ratios, compliance aware. cost control, and innovation.

Whilst in London RIB provided me with a comfortable flat in Mount Street Mayfair, very handy for our favourite butchers Allens. Most weekends we were invited by friends to stay in the country. Nick and Valda Embiricos were great fun to stay with. Nick had just discovered bull shots. Rumours were strongly denied we kept the makers of Campbell's consommé in overtime!

Gawaine and Margot Baillie had just built a modern country house near Warninglid in West Sussex. Everything was state of the art, done with great taste. Margot was a brilliant hostess and, through her butler and staff, managed the house superbly. Highly intelligent, she did tend to dominate the dinner table and, for some reason would affectionately address Gawaine as "rabbit." Gawaine was always keen for me to see his stamp collection and to discuss two of his business interests. These were a Mercedes Benz dealership and an engineering factory he owned in Burgess Hill. Gawaine's idea of a barbecue was to have the chef do the outdoor cooking in white apron and toque. I recall in 1966 Gawaine wrote to me in glowing terms to say how pleased he was to have become engaged to Margot in Nantucket. He said he expected that I would be next!

Hubert Martineau was occasionally in London in his suite at Claridges. He came over to renew his Rolls Royce every other year with Jack Barclay. He invited Lesley and I to stay at his chalet in Switzerland for a long weekend. We were duly met at Geneva airport by his chauffeur, who took us to meet Hubert at the Beau Rivage hotel. Hubert explained that he had just suffered a bad attack of breathlessness and could not go up the mountains. Would we mind staying at the Beau

Rivage as his guests. Because of ill health Hubert was never to go up to St. Moritz again. He sold his chalet and handed over Presidency of The St Moritz Tobogganing Club and Cresta Run to Gunther Sachs. His stories of taking cricket teams to Egypt at his own expense, and of his friendship with Little Willie (The Kaiser)

With Hubert Martineau and his new wife.

in St Moritz after WW1 were fascinating. Our dear friends Martin and Aline Parsons, and their sons Rupert and Richard, had returned to London after a long spell in Australia. Martin had inherited a grand house in Lennox Gardens from an aunt. The inheritance was a life changer after their modest bungalow in Melbourne. Martin and Aline were indefatigable entertainers. At one of their dinner parties I am told, Lesley and Martin's godfather the writer Harold Acton, consumed quite a few bottles of Chateau Margaux between them, while trying to outdo each other in praise of Italy. Being godfather to Martin, stemmed from

Martin's father having been Harold Acton's fag at Eton. Harold Acton belonged to an effete clique of wealthy literati living in Italy. He owned a grand Palacio in Florence, which, upon his death, was bequeathed to an American university "a shroud has no pockets!"

Hong Kong 1975

Having joined RIB HK it was arranged that I should meet the HK representative of NMR.

As he was visiting London I invited him to drinks at my friend Martin Parsons house in Lennox Gardens.

I think he was a bit disconcerted by the grandeur of Lord Rosse's son's London house and was clearly not too comfortable with our meeting. There was no doubt he saw me as a threat to his position in Hong Kong. He would obviously have preferred a less experienced and more pliable appointee. I was not impressed with him, not least because he had virtually no banking and little business experience. To his credit, he had worked for the foreign office and had received an OBE for his services.

On my arrival in Hong Kong he did not give me the courtesy of being met and the small bedroom provided at The Hilton Hotel was woefully inadequate for a family of three. Worse was to follow when, at his instigation, I was provided with a cramped run down two bedroom flat in Wanchai. As I saw it, reasonably prestigious accommodation was vital in promoting the business of RIB. I wasted no time in finding more suitable accommodation for entertaining. The Mackinnon Mackenzie P&O house on the Peak came up for rent and I was able to secure it for RIB much to the chagrin of the Rothschild representative. My wife and I gave many drinks and dinner parties at the house in order to promote the business of RIB. When Evelyn and Jacob Rothschild visited Hong Kong a reception was given for them at The Peninsula Hotel. Hubert

Martineau, one of the guests and a personal friend of mine, was a valued client of N M Rothschild. At the reception he button holed Evelyn R to complain that he was unhappy with the replacement of the long time NMR representative who usually visited him annually in Switzerland.

Hubert M had inherited a vast fortune from his wife Maude Guggenheim some of which was wealth managed by NMR London. The morning after the reception, Tom Stonor, myself, and the two Rothschilds were in a meeting in my office when my secretary interrupted to say Mr Martineau was on the telephone and wanted to speak to Mr Rothschild. She was asked which Mr Rothschild? She came back and said "the one he upset last night! "I was able to placate Hubert by advising him to buy physical gold and HSBC shares. He did very well out of both investments.

The unwelcome takeover of The Dairy Farm Co by Jardine Matheson was defended by N M Rothschild. Rodney Leach flew out from NMR London, but even his then impressive embryonic corporate finance talents could not save The Dairy Farm Co. It was not too long before, that Rodney had come down from Oxford with a good degree,and a disconcerting full head of shoulder length hair, and attitude.

Henry Keswick, Jardine's taipan, was miffed to find that the last act of the ousted Dairy Farm Chairman was to authorise a huge coffer emptying defence fee, payable to NMR. In later life Rodney became Lord Fairford, and the eminence grise of Jardine.

23 NOV 1973

H CHINA MORNING POST

A cocktail party was recently held by Mr A. F. McCardle (right) Director of Rothschild Intercontinental Bank Finance (HK) Ltd, and his wife (second from left) at the Peninsula in honour of The Hon Thomas Stoner (left) Managing Director of Rothschild Intercontinental Bank Limited and Chairman of Rothschild Intercontinental Bank Finance (HK) Limited, and his wife (second from right).

When the Hong Kong NMR representative was away on a visit to London it came to my attention that he had been sending unauthenticated telegrams to NMR in London instructing them to make third party payments and implement investment trading orders. I pointed out to London the danger of acting on unauthenticated telegrams and insisted a secure authenticating system was implemented. This did not please the Rothschild representative who was deviously making it his business to persuade NMR London that, as long as I was in Hong Kong, HSBC would be biased against Rothschild. These machiavellian overtures had no foundation whatsoever. I am sure HSBC had more to do than fret about my departure, or worry about competition, if any, from Rothschilds.

Host. Rothschild Intercontinental Bank reception Hong Kong.

It became painfully apparent that The Rothschild rep and myself could not work together. At a poolside party given by my friend Michael Uttley I accidentally dived into the pool at the shallow end and sustained a fracture to my fourth vertebrae, medically a broken neck. As a result I was away from the office for some weeks, during which time The Rothschild rep persuaded RIB and NMR London to believe that, as he and I could not work together, I should leave. Matters came to a head on my return to the office and I was ultimately persuaded to resign. So it was, that having abandoned my career with HSBC, I was now out of a job with a broken neck to boot! Not surprisingly, at that time, career wise, I very much regretted having left HSBC, where I belonged.

Not too long after my departure from RIB I was vindicated when it was discovered that the Rothschild Representative was guilty of gross misconduct.

His misdeeds caused Rothschild London senior management to urgently fly out to Hong Kong to confront him. Having harmed my career and tarnished the reputation of Rothschild in Hong Kong, the unmasked rogue fled the colony.

Unforeseen internecine squabbling between N M Rothschild and RIB over business on offer and other concerns seriously handicapped RIB's prospects. I was not surprised to see RIB eventually being absorbed by American Express. Tom Stonor, who impressed me greatly as a negotiator and administrator, became Lord Camoys. He went on to join Barclays, served as Lord Chamberlain, and was an adviser to the Vatican Holy Sea on finance matters.

CHAPTER EIGHTEEN
Australia 1975 1993

Following my departure from RIB in Hong Kong I decided to return to Australia. Euro Pacific Finance Corporation Ltd was looking for an assistant General Manager to take charge of their Sydney office. Following discussions, I decided to accept the job offer. Euro Pacific Finance Corporation Ltd (Euro Pacific) was a consortium of international banks engaged in a limited range of profitable financial dealings, but without the benefit of a banking licence. The shareholders of Euro Pacific were some of the biggest financial institutions in the world, being Canadian Imperial Bank of Commerce, Midland Bank, Fuji Bank, Deutsche Bank, United California Bank, Amsterdam Rotterdam Bank, Societe General, and the Commercial Bank of Australia. All of the overseas shareholders wanted a presence in Australia, whilst hoping for a banking licence in due course. To assist me I had a number of expatriate staff seconded from the overseas shareholder banks to the office in Sydney. They were particularly useful in obtaining business from their respective ethnic corporate contacts in Australia. Tragically Alfred Herrhausen, the Chairman of Deutsche Bank, was assassinated in Germany, just before he was due to attend a Euro-Pacific board meeting in Australia. A huge loss to banking.

I made periodic visits to Melbourne. These visits were usually to attend lending committee meetings for business emanating from Sydney.

Financier. My office in Sydney.

I was amazed to learn, years later, that one of the lending committee members turned out to be a cross dresser who, dressed as a woman, was found with his throat cut, but alive, in Melbourne. During my visits to Melbourne I much enjoyed visiting my old clubs. I used the Melbourne club on a reciprocal basis, and was a member of the Naval and Military club, and the Savage Club. In order to hone my public speaking skills I joined a debating group for a time. At their once a fortnight meetings the emphasis was on improving diction, confidence, and delivery. With the benefit of these teachings I was fortunate to win the American Chamber of Commerce, Sydney, Speaker of the year contest. My improved public speaking skills were also helpful in an ABC Four Corners televised interview.

In 1974, Not too long after joining Euro Pacific, Lesley and I were invited to Japan to the launching of Nick Embiricos's new family tanker. The launching was a great success and we enjoyed the hospitality of Mitsui & Co the ship builders. In 1978 I took sabbatical leave to attend University in Hawaii. I successfully applied for a place in a Harvard Business Course at the university of Hawaii and obtained a diploma in Pacific Management Program Studies.

Student. University of Hawaii.

I took the children on holiday to Fiji in the early 1990's. Whilst there, we all had to run the gauntlet of a phalanx of giant crabs with menacing claws blocking our way to our bungalow in the grounds of the hotel. It was dangerous to swim in the sea, owing to numerous venomous sea snakes swimming around like old school ties. I also took the children on holiday to the Whitsundays Islands in the Great Barrier Reef. Swimming amongst the unforgettable coral we enjoyed having our feet nibbled by shoals of tiny fish, and the opportunity of hand feeding a huge grouper under water.

During the mid 1980's I was included in a group of bankers to tour the Australian mines. The mining industry was booming with exports going mainly to Japan and China. All the bankers participating had to make their way individually to Perth, where, as a group, we were addressed by the tour conductor. There were 14 participants in the expedition. Out of a hat we were each allocated a "mate". In my case my mate turned out to be a likeable Japanese. He was a senior banker with The Industrial Bank of Japan. He was surprised to learn that I had spent 4 years in Japan and spoke some Japanese. As a posse of bankers our transport was a squadron of 4 light aircraft. We would take off early each morning and make our way around Western Australia. Our first stop was Kalgoorlie. We had a tour of the gold mines and stayed overnight in a rather rickety old colonial hotel. The breakfast menu was either mince or steak. From there we flew on in our 'light' planes to the Pilbara to see the iron ore excavations at Mount Tom Price. The sheer size of the mining machinery was breath taking. The height of the wheels on one piece of machinery was over twenty feet.

Australian mining tour.

There was a makeshift golf course fashioned out of compacted iron ore dust. On a conventional golf course one would expect to replace the turf. In the Pilbara, because of the extreme hardness of the iron ore fairway, it was more usual to replace a golf club! We flew on to Wapit Island to visit an oil well coming to the end of it's viable use. Oil was extracted from a depth becoming no longer viable. It was interesting to learn that sea water was being pumped into the well so that the oil basin would float upward on the sea water thus allowing easier, and cheaper, extraction. From there we flew on to Broome. We stayed in a hotel developed by Lord McAlpine and were invited by the nurses to a dance at the local hospital. My Japanese "mate" wanted to pay his respects to the many Japanese pearl divers who had lost their lives over the years diving off Broome. I went along with him to the Japanese graveyard. It was quite sad to see how many had died so young. Next day it was off to Kununurra. On the way, we landed in a field in the middle of nowhere, to be refuelled by monks in sandals and brown hassocks. They seemed to manhandle the large Avgas containers with ease. Kununurra had a large Aboriginal population. There was not very much employment for them, and their cash welfare benefit was mostly spent on booze. I was shown a gigantic mound of empty beer bottles I was told some day the mounds will be bigger than the pyramids! We were told about a local drink called the "leg opener "or "bush champagne" it was made from methylated spirits with a pinch of baking soda. I'm afraid not quite my taste. I would prefer the usual Crystal or a good vintage Krug. Diamonds had only recently been discovered at the Argyle diamond mine. The mine was already becoming known for it's pink diamonds. All of us enjoyed seeing Lake Argyle. It was much bigger than I had expected. Geikie gorge was interesting, although it was disappointing not to see any crocodiles, but we did see lots of Galahs, a native parrot. Bauxite is used to make aluminium. In one area we visited, bauxite was lying around over a huge area. All one had to do was pick it up. For me this hugely interesting expedition ended in Darwin, from where I flew back to Sydney on a commercial flight.

My youngest daughter Skye was born in Sydney in 1976. At the time we were living in Cremorne, in a house overlooking a wooded Sydney harbour inlet.

In 1979 we moved to Victoria Road Bellevue Hill, our family home until I left Australia in 1993.

I suffered a severe heart attack in the office in 1986. The speed at which I was attended to by paramedic and taken to hospital undoubtedly saved my life. After recovery I returned to the office for a time before being persuaded to take up less stressful, but more rewarding work, managing the family textile business.

Eventually, under Prime Minister Keating, Euro Pacific's overseas shareholders were granted banking licences. Thus, the raison d'être for Euro Pacific evaporated. Looking back, I enjoyed my role at Euro-Pacific where I valued the combination of job satisfaction combined with a happy family life.

The family textile business, InMaterial Pty Ltd, was growing rapidly. I contributed more capital to enable the business to profitably expand into it's own premises in Surry Hills. We bought a commercial building which provided us with offices, warehouse space, cutting room and despatch facilities.

The business was the wholesale distribution of a wide range of furnishing fabrics. The materials were mainly sourced from Europe, Japan, USA, and China. In the case of fabrics imported from America it meant a yearly buying visit to New York. There we would call on convertors. Convertors were usually Jewish owned and were the link between the mills and the wholesalers. The converters would buy straight from the mills and sell on to wholesalers. We would visit their showrooms to choose patterns we believed would sell profitably in Australia. In order to obtain exclusivity in Australia for a particular pattern, we had to order a minimum quantity. The order could be drawn down in tranches spread over an agreed period. Initially, we would order 2 or 3 bolts of fabric to be air freighted to Australia so that pattern books and show room drops could be made up. The sample books were then distributed to our retail customers so that they, in turn, could take orders from their customers. Some retailers objected to paying for samples. However, very often they would agree to pay for a sample if the cost of the sample was refunded from their first order (of over 5 meters) from that sample.

American printed cottons were one of our more profitable stock lines. Indent hotel contracts were profitable with often little effort. If one of our exclusive curtain/bedspread coordinates was specified, the fabric would be shipped direct to the maker without our having to even handle the shipment through our warehouse. In the case of stock fabrics, almost invariably we would ultimately end up with some unsold remnant stock. These unsold remnants were a drag on profits. To make space in the warehouse the unsold stock was sold to jobbers at a very heavily discounted price, or left with them on a consignment basis.

In addition to InMaterial Pty Lid, The Knightsbridge Silver Co Pty Ltd was also family owned. I found my new role as an entrepreneur very rewarding and a satisfying change from some of the constraints of banking. Best of all, I didn't always have to wear a suit! In the early 1980s we rented our flat in Point Piper to Patti LuPone who was playing the lead role in "Evita." She gave a drinks party at which I met a young budding Australian actor called Mel Gibson. He later turned out to be a Hollywood super star. About that time, in recognition of Australian film revenue potential, the Australian Tax Office allowed some tax concessions to film production investors. These initiatives undoubtedly encouraged Australian film production to flourish. Some scenes in the TV drama Tanamiror Lion of Singapore were filmed in our drawing room at Bellevue Hill. It was a huge disruption with cables everywhere. We were, however, handsomely rewarded for the inconvenience. At about the same time our neighbour, Martin Sharp, became obsessed with making a film about Tiny Tim the entertainer. I suspect most of the footage ended up on the cutting room floor.

The walled garden in The Melbourne Club was a very agreeable place to have pre lunch or pre dinner drinks in the summer. Next door at the Naval and Military Club bar, I often enjoyed the company of Ken Cole and Bill Robertson. Ken worked in the oil industry for Caltex. Bill had served in a Highland Regiment as GSO 1 at the Normandy landings and was highly decorated.

He was, for a time, head of Australian intelligence, until he had a falling out with PM Gough Whitlam over the Timor uprising. John Doble was known for his Sunday morning drinks parties in South Yarra. He was a well known man about town, and had dealings with BHP. Martin Parsons could mimic John to a T, much to everyone's amusement.

Melbourne social life mainly revolved around dinner parties, business receptions, and cocktail parties. Weekends were often spent away in the country, with sometimes limited ski-ing in the winter at Thredbo. My friend Chic Murray became Governor of Victoria when he retired from the Australian navy, having achieved admiral rank. He and his charming wife, very kindly invited Lesley and I to dinner at Government house, where only the four of us dined in grand style,

Over dinner, Chic explained to me how he personally painted a window in a Government house bedroom in readiness for Prince Charles. He said he did it to save money, because of very tight budget constraints.

When excusing himself to go to the loo, he would often say, he was going to shake hands with the unemployed!

DIY Renovater Belleview Hill Sydney house.

Following my darling Lesley's tragic death, and my open heart bypass surgery in 1990, I decided to sell the businesses and retire to the UK, thus ending my overseas banking and entrepreneurial roles.

CHAPTER NINETEEN

Bank Woes

Reason for my resignation from HSBC

In the early seventies there was discontent amongst some of the senior foreign staff facing retirement. The mandatory retirement age of 55 or 30 years service whichever came first was causing some hardship. There were even a few distressing cases of pensioners and pensioner's widows, not being able to manage financially. Inflation had eroded the value of pensions. Compared with the normal retirement age of 65 there were simply not enough earning years for some, like myself, who married late, to accrue adequate retirement provision.

In a bygone age, the mandatory young retirement age was put in place in recognition of the health consequences of serving long tours in tropical climates, no air travel, no air conditioning, and poor medical care.

Uncharacteristically, the Bank was lamentably slow in addressing this very serious problem in a changing world.

In these circumstances, and with huge regret, I was constrained to accept an offer of adequately superannuated employment elsewhere.

I was, dismayed to be told that following my resignation, my pension benefit, earned over many years, indeed decades, was to be forfeited.

Ever since, I have felt deprived concerning my loss of pension benefits for services rendered. In this respect, it pains me to feel critical of the Bank, who it seems would prefer me, and others, to suffer in dutiful silence.

I am sure few would condone the action of a highly profitable Bank voiding the reasonable pension expectations of very long serving staff who have voluntary resigned for good reasons. Many believe, as I do, that the preservation of an individual's pension benefits is sacrosanct. It beggars belief that pension forfeiture can be so arrogantly used to satisfy the prejudices of a miffed Executive Director. Voiding long service pension credit is, to my mind, tantamount to theft, or at the very least, sharp practice. As a legal issue, it is debatable, as a moral issue, also in my view, indefensible.

The small group who did resign, and on whom the Bank had placed considerable reliance and responsibilities, were quite the opposite of persons guilty of misconduct. There is not the slightest question of misconduct for any one of them. My pension benefit was not handed over to me with gratitude after 22 years of dutiful and trusted service, but confiscated simply because at age 42, with a young family, I needed to carry on working beyond the Bank's (premature) mandatory retirement age. I had a responsibility to provide adequately for my family in retirement.

As an HSBC shareholder, I would applaud the Board if, for the sake of fairness, they were to review the questionable treatment of the small number of long service resigners who's accrued pension benefits were so unjustly denied.

The Bank did settle my provident fund, amounting to a derisory £6000 almost half of which was my own contribution. I sometimes wonder if I would be able to protect the Bank in circumstances where I was subpoenaed under a compelling jurisdiction to reveal my knowledge of the Bank's litany of wrongdoings, much of which is, sadly, already in the public domain.

After my resignation, I remained a member of The Pigtail Club, since renamed The Wayfoong Club. Almost all my colleagues on the foreign staff were members of the Club. The Club was formed to foster good fellowship amongst both serving and ex foreign and home staff. The annual dinner usually held at the Royal Overseas League Club house presented a good opportunity to catch up with many old friends. After the annual dinner I enjoyed sometimes taking a few close friends over to Boodles for cigars, brandy, and reminiscences. In other years, John Gray would do the post prandial honours at the Oriental Club.

Since I left the Bank, from time to time, I have enjoyed catching up with some of the HSBC luminaries such as, Jake Saunders, Mike Sandberg, Willie Purves and John Bond, either at the Wayfoong dinner or on other occasions. I first met John Bond in 1967 on his posting to Bangkok office where I was the just married accountant standing in for David Jaques. Stephen Green and I never served together. We did meet by chance at a dinner party in Rye. At the dinner, I was surprised when he told me he was ordained and worked for HSBC, and even more surprised when, in response to my asking what his job was, he casually mentioned he had just been appointed Group Chairman. He was to prove a worthy successor to John Bond, and was honoured by a well deserved peerage.

My resignation was a protest at the Bank's recalcitrance in changing the out dated retirement rules causing hardship. My resignation was not accepted by the Chairman with regret and understanding as I had hoped, but rather, on the grounds that it caused some inconvenience, with gratuitous hostility and pension confiscation. In his letter to me acknowledging my resignation, he complained of my short notice and my intention to work in Hong Kong with another bank. Not a word about my contribution to the Bank's profits. I explained that after decades of devotion to the Bank, I agonised for weeks in deciding about leaving. I apologised for the short notice, due to my ultimate decision io resign coming almost at the end of my leave. As for my joining another bank, he would surely be aware that the Bank does not have a monopoly in Hong Kong, and that almost every bank in the world Is there in competition. I would certainly not be revealing any of HSBC secrets to other banks, and, in any case, I had not worked in Hong Kong for the past seven years. In his letter, the Chairman avoided mention of the raison d'être for my resignation, that being a protest at the outmoded age related retirement rules. Surely not a reason for pension forfeiture.

For the sake of others, I am pleased to say the reason for my resignation was a wake up call to the Bank. Not long afterwards the out dated retirement rules were changed for the benefit of all serving, and for those to follow.

My Forfeited HSBC Pension Benefit

During my 22 years service, voluntary resignation of a Foreign Staff member was extremely rare. On joining the Foreign Staff of the Bank, all recruits, were required to join the Foreign Staff Retirement Benefits Scheme. The superannuation scheme was non contributory. Benefits were earned as part of ones emoluments. As a young recruit it never occurred to me that, in due course, the pension scheme would become, to my mind, not so much a golden handcuff, as more of an employment shackle.

Cynically designed to inhibit valued staff from leaving the Bank, compliant pension fund trustees could be unilaterally directed to deny earned pension benefit credits to a member resigning voluntarily.

To my mind this questionable draconian rule, if resorted to, is surely grossly unfair in the case of those with very long profit earning devoted service, resigning for good reasons.

At a time of plummeting HSBC share prices, it saddens me greatly, to see that in recent times, the Bank's once impeccable reputation has been sullied. One reads about complicity in money laundering, tax evasion, a catalogue of legal issues, and even bonuses so large they have to be hidden from colleagues. I have nothing against large bonuses, if the amounts are realistically contractually linked to an agreed percentage of attributable profits, and subject to claw back. Given the Bank's vast profits, I also have nothing against breathtaking pension pots, provided they are performance linked. The forfeiture of long service pension credits is quite another matter, and to which I am vehemently opposed.

The Bank promotes the notion that it is a fair employer. Yet, in my view, that is debatable. For example, in the case of voluntary resignation, can the withholding of long service retirement benefits, earned diligently and dutifully over decades, be considered fair? I think not. As a shareholder, the combined talents of a phalanx of twenty well paid directors gives me some confidence in the Bank's ongoing guidance. As always, I have the greatest respect and admiration for HSBC staff at every level.

In the present compliance sensitive banking environment there are many challenges, not least the pressures of competition from non bank, non regulated, high tech, financial institutions. The trend to disintermediation is also a concern amongst banks, but, against that, HSBC has never been short of innovation. These days it is not all bad news for the banks. If they can borrow from Central Bank windows at very low interest rates, and lend out the funds to credit card borrowers at 24.7% or higher, business can't be too bad. Profitably funding credit card borrowers, from no cost money on current account, is even better!

I wonder who benefits when the Bank unilaterally confiscates long service pension funds?

It is breathtaking to see the Bank paying out billions of dollars in fines or compensation for wrongdoing, yet is so intransigent and dismissive in addressing pension injustices concerning it's own staff, to my mind, the worst wrongdoing of all!

Some in the Bank may well be disappointed to see that I have raised the contentious subject of retirement benefit forfeiture. If so, perhaps they might reflect on my disappointment on being told that, after decades of dutiful service, and the debilitating consequences of contracting dysentery and dengue fever in the Bank's service, my reward was pension confiscation.

Conclusion

In the absence of misconduct, confiscation of very long service retirement benefits is, to my mind, morally wrong, and therefor is open to challenge.

The confiscation of my accrued retirement benefits, hard earned year after year, decade after decade, as part of my emoluments, was a huge disappointment to me. Whilst disbursing breath taking benefits to some, the Bank attempts to keep faith with this punitive and petty act of ingratitude on the grounds that the fine print in the retirement benefits rules allows the Trustees the option of confiscation in cases of voluntary resignation, regardless of length of service. To my mind, invoking this questionable rule is an injustice , especially in cases of long and very long satisfactory service, and does not sit well with the Bank's self proclaimed image of being a "fair" employer. As well as ignoring pension portability protocol, the Bank may well argue that the rule is there as a disincentive to dissuade valued senior management from leaving. If that is so, surely it would be more equitable to retain staff by offering incentives rather than the threat of punitive pension confiscation. If this long outstanding issue continues to be left unresolved, it may well be that long service accrued pension confiscation could emerge for justice, being yet another item in the Bank's inglorious litany of known wrongdoings.

Apart from the Bank's clandestine role as a serial staff pension confiscator, I am, as an encomiast, a devoted admirer of the Bank as a financial institution. On the other hand, I strongly condemn the practice of long service retirement benefit confiscation as morally wrong, no matter how much the Bank attempts to legitimise the theft, whilst, at the same time, professing sympathy with those it has dispossessed.

On a more positive note, I like to think that, by resigning for the good reasons I did, my legacy to the Bank was to sound a wake up call, prompting the Bank to introduce long overdue improvements to terms and conditions for those of my colleagues who continued in service, and who did so with such brilliant results.

CHAPTER TWENTY

Wardour

Having sold the business in Sydney and let my house, I found myself relocated in London looking for accommodation. An advertisement in Country Life caught my eye. It was advertising an apartment to rent in Wardour Castle, Wiltshire. Having just bought a used BMW 7 series, I thought I would give it a run and drive down to Wiltshire to view the apartment. The new Wardour castle is a country house built in 1776 for the Arundel family. The old Wardour castle was partly destroyed in the civil war and is a feature in the new castle grounds. One of the outstanding features of Wardour castle is the rotunda staircase designed by architect James Paine.

The unfurnished apartment to let was on the top floor of the main building accessed by a passenger lift. The drawing room was vast. There was a row of casement windows on one side overlooking the east wing and the grounds beyond. A French style chimney piece containing a swan nest fire basket was at one end and there was ample space for dining at the other end. The kitchen was modern and spacious. There were two large bedrooms. Each bedroom had a superb Carrara marble en suite bathroom with Czech and Speake fittings and walk in marble encased shower. I made up my mind on the spot and signed a lease for three years. I enjoyed the opportunity of decorating the apartment and became a frequent bidder at Lots Road, Christies South Kensington, and Wooley and Wooley in Salisbury in my quest for furnishings. Eventually, I put together an eclectic lot of antiques together with a modern glass dining table and some acceptable, if not outstanding, art. I found a very good French Aubusson carpet at Christies. I bought it quite cheaply as nobody wanted it because of it's vast size. It suited the centre of the drawing room perfectly. On it, I placed a rather good French kingwood and ormolu bureau plat, also bought at Christies. There was a nice walk between the new castle and the old one. At a certain time of the year there was an outstanding show of woodland blue bells to pass through.

I could not have wished for better neighbours at Wardour. Peter and Elaine Rawlinson had one wing and Robert and Jan Churchill had the wing on the opposite side. Nigel Tuersley and his family occupied the grand principal rooms in the central part of the castle. There was also a very pleasant Danish couple in an apartment on the top floor.

The chapel of all saints in the castle is a neo classical masterpiece. To attend, all I had to do was leave my front door, go downstairs, and I was there. Although Scottish Presbyterian, I felt quite at home with the Roman Catholic service. When in Rome - I simply felt we were all Christians worshiping together. If in Salisbury I would occasionally drop in to admire the cathedral. One quiet week day while sitting in a pew, I experienced an overwhelming almost surreal, feeling of total peace and contentment. The sensation didn't last very long but the memory will always remain with me.

Peter and Elaine Rawlinson were very hospitable neighbours. Peter would occasionally ask me to join him for a pub lunch. He said he missed the lunches he used to enjoy when he was a member of the HSBC London Committee. I was fascinated to hear about some of his experiences when he was Attorney General. Elaine had a great talent for interior decorating. Her wing of the castle was testament to her brilliant flair and unfailing good taste. Peter's eightieth birthday was celebrated at a luncheon in a marquee at old Wardour Castle. It was a splendid affair beautifully organised by Elaine. Geoffrey Howe gave, as expected, a very witty speech. While queuing for our table I passed the time in small talk with Conrad Black the Canadian newspaper tycoon and his wife.

Years later, I recall being ushered to my seat in the Guards chapel by Michael Howard at Peter Rawlinson's memorial. Peter might well have become Lord Chancellor but for Lord Hailsham sitting on the wool sack, according to some, for far too long. I happened to be in Sydney when sadly Lady Hailsham died tragically in a riding accident in Centennial park.

After I moved to Wardour Castle, I frequently drove up to London with occasional trips to Scotland for salmon fishing with my nephew Nick Clark. Zinnia (Lady Judd) my companion at that time was an eventing judge. We drove to most horse shows where she was judging including, Burghley, Hickstead, and most notably The Royal Windsor Horse Show. Zinnia persuaded me to sponsor an event at the Royal Windsor show. I presented a small cup to the winner of a side saddle event. Afterwards, all the sponsors were invited to meet the Queen at a reception. It was the second time that week I had the honour of meeting the Queen and Prince Phillip. A few days earlier I had escorted Zinnia to a dinner to mark the Queen's 50th wedding anniversary at Windsor.

Two Australian women were in line at the horse show reception to meet the Queen. It later turned out that they were cheating the horse fraternity, including Zinnia, out of thousands of pounds while pretending they were millionaire event sponsors. Even I was taken in as they persuaded me to introduce them to Coutts bank. They were later jailed.

After horse trials at Burghley, Reresby and Penelope Sitwell invited Zinnia and I to stay the weekend at Renishaw their house in Derbyshire.

Sir Reresby who had a great sense of humour wore his dressing gown the whole weekend. After the Sitwells we dropped in briefly to have tea with Zinnia's friends the nearby McCorquodales. We also visited the Hulses, Eddy and Verity. Their splendid house was originally a grant to Sir Edward Hulse's ancestor in 1739. He was physician to Queen Anne, George 1 and George 11. Verity did occasional voluntary work at the V&A whilst Eddy, amongst other things, looked after the family collection of important ancestral portrait paintings, often on loan to overseas galleries.

After a time I found I was spending most of my time seeing Zinnia at her flat in Lennox Gardens and was hardly ever at Wardour. So it seemed to make sense not to renew the Wardour lease. Instead, I bought a flat in Egerton Gardens, Knightsbridge.

Not very long afterwards Zinnia was rushed to King George V hospital, where tragically she died of advanced breast cancer. Her funeral was well attended. Afterwards, her life was remembered over champagne in the garden of Bill Shand-Kidd's house.

Londoner. Parked in Belgrave Square.

Everyone gathered in groups, some remembering Zinnia, and others, in their grief, talking about everything and anything but the deceased. Without the assistance of my friend Frank Plugge I could not have attended Zinnia's funeral. About two days before the funeral, I had a bad fall on some stairs in my flat. I fell awkwardly on my right knee and managed to crawl into bed in great pain. The next morning, I somehow managed to limp in to the A&E section of Westminster hospital on the King's road. I was put on an operating table where, without anaesthetic, an enormous syringe was used to drain the fluid from my swollen knee. The pain was absolutely excruciating! On the day of the funeral Frank drove me, and I managed to hobble around with the aid of a walking stick. Some time later, Zinnia's two sons arranged a memorial reception for their mama at the guards officers mess in Birdcage Walk.

About this time I met a most attractive American lady called Marianne. At least I thought she was American but she was in fact

Dutch. She was a widow, and had lived in San Francisco for many years with her American husband. We enjoyed a very correct relationship for some months before I had to go to Australia and she departed to stay in Spain.

Marianne in party mode San Francisco and
outdoors at Suvretta House St. moritz

After a time Zinnia's friend Eugenie and I started going out together. In due course it made sense for me to let my flat in Egerton Gardens and share Eugenie's house in Belgravia. Later, Eugenie bought a house in Rye where we were together for some years. I enjoyed living in Rye with it's endless drinks and dinner parties, with nearly always the same mostly charming and amusing people. Eugenie was very popular in the Rye social scene. We had a large circle of friends including such luminaries as, Paul Blomfield and his charming sister Priscilla, Anne and Basil Phillips, Tia and David Russell, and Lady Marjory Murray. At the annual meeting of the Rye Preservation Society I would occasionally find myself standing outside the town hall having a cigarette in company with Donald Sinden the actor. Donald was a brilliant raconteur and story teller, and it was a great treat to hear his jokes over a furtive cigarette. One of his jokes, recited in a strong Yorkshire accent, was about a bunch of WW1 Yorkshire factory girls having a group photo taken. The photographer was out front adjusting his camera on a tripod under a blanket. One of the girls nudged her friend and asked "Ee what's he doing under that blanket?" Her friend replied "Ee I think he's trying to focus." The reply was "What, all of us?" Another quickie was "Did you hear about the woman who fell asleep in Hyde Park? She woke up with a heavy dew on her! It seemed as if we were all play acting roles in Benson's Mapp and Lucia scenarios. After a time Eugenie and I bought a flat in Chelsea and divided our time between Rye and London, interspersed with holiday trips abroad. On a visit to Shanghai, we were able to see inside the HSBC old office on the bund. It all seemed like a time warp with lots of art nouveaux architectural touches in evidence.

Eugenie in St. Barts

It was in Rye where I decided to change my Bentley for a more sedate Rolls Royce silver spirit. The car was midnight blue, with cream leather upholstery. The cavernous boot was well suited for picnics at Ascot and for booze cruising to Calais. In Calais, the French super market Carrefour had a surprisingly good fine wine section. I once found a rare vintage bottle of Petruse for €300.

Given the cost I reluctantly decided it would be better appreciated by a wine connoisseur, and at the same time I might make a profit. Eugenie's son Charlie Vere Nicoll and his wife Mandie had an interest in the very exclusive Hotel Isle de France in St Barts. Eugenie and I had just returned from a holiday there, and it occurred to me that the sommelier might like to add my hard to get Petruse to his wine list. Charlie was good enough to agree and, eventually, the bottle was sold in the restaurant at a handsome profit, no one being more pleased than the customer who bought it.

It was in St. Barts, in church, I found myself standing beside the controversial American Bishop Gene Robinson. He was on holiday and was attending Sunday morning prayers as an ordinary member of the congregation. We were nearly all casually dressed in short sleeved shirts and shorts. After the service, conducted by Eugenie's son Charlie Vere-Nicoll, we enjoyed customary refreshments in the shaded church yard. I found Gene Robinson an engaging conversationalist and, in my view, a very able and charismatic Bishop.

I had some very comfortable drives in the Rolls to and from Scotland and, once, to Switzerland, to stay in my apartment in Montreux. On visits to Scotland, my nephew Nick Clark, was good enough to organise some occasional salmon fishing. On one of these fishing expeditions I was lucky enough to catch a good sized salmon. We were fishing on the Stincher, a spate river in south Ayrshire.

Angler. Salmon fishing in Scotland.

The next day I had the fish packed in ice and motored with it to London. En route, I was ambling along at a mere 85 mph on the A66 when I was flagged down by a police patrol car. The policeman took a dim view of my speed. I was fined, and lost points for the offence. On arrival at my flat in London, I was dismayed to find there wasn't a big enough fish kettle in the kitchen in which to poach the salmon. With guests coming, my salmon was in danger of being a non starter. Someone suggested that I should prepare the salmon for cooking and then place it in the dish washing machine, having first double wrapped it in foil. With great apprehension, I followed the instructions and, without adding detergent, switched on the dishwasher at my usual setting. I was absolutely amazed and delighted to find the salmon, perfectly cooked at the end of the dishwasher programme.

I was very pleased when my old friend Edward Scott turned up in London. Unlike myself, engaged in the pursuit of selfish pleasures and amusements, Edward was to take up his appointment as Chairman of John Swire & Son in London, and was looking for accommodation. Over dinner at Whites, it was arranged that Edward would have the use of my flat (for a consideration) whilst I was away in Australia for a few weeks. The arrangement worked out well. Afterwards, Edward found a flat in Westminster overlooking the river. In due course, he and Angela, his new wife, found a country house at Ampney Crucis. It was there and at the London Clinic, I last saw Edward before he died, tragically, of cancer. During my visit to Australia, I had to undergo an operation for a prostate blockage. The operation was performed by a brilliant urologist and was highly successful. Apparently during the operating procedure there was some drama with my heart and breathing misbehaving. When I regained consciousness in intensive care, the nurses told me I had given them a scare. At one point they said they thought they had lost me! Sometime later, I was hugely relieved to find the operation had not affected my ability to "caper nimbly in a lady's chamber to the lascivious pleasing of a lute!." I am quoting here, in archaic language, from a soliloquy excerpt in Shakespeare's Richard 111. There is, of course, the old prostate road sign joke "Dover for the continent, Eastbourne for the incontinent!"

In 2004 I went to Australia once again for an operation. This time for open heart surgery to replace three of the four grafts I had done in 1990. The operation was again very successful. The surgeon told me my heart per se was strong and healthy. The problem was cholesterol related blockages in the arteries. In 1990 the surgeon had used arteries harvested from my right leg. It was subsequently discovered that arteries taken from the chest worked better. In my last operation they took arteries from my arms as well, as a sort of belt and braces contingency measure, in case the chest arteries were unusable in mid operation. Another good medic story was about an elderly lady on being asked how she was replied, "Would you like to hear an organ recital?"

After a time the Rolls started giving trouble. Some rust appeared on the body and there was also expensive transmission repairs. I decided to trade in the rolls for a Mercedes CLK 430.

My friend John Gray had just retired from being Chairman of The Honkong and Shanghai Banking Corporation in Hong Kong. He and I had great fun driving out to Switzerland. On one occasion we had a memorable dinner with some exceptionally good Montrachet in the village of Montrachet. John also joined Pat Tudor as my house guests in Scotland. We enjoyed some good golf at Turnberry and motoring around Argyle. Sadly, both John and Pat were to die within a year of each other. I was in Hong Kong expecting to have lunch with John when I received the devastating news that he had died that morning. At his memorial service in London, I had to summon reserves of sang froid in order to keep a dry eye whilst listening to Willie Purves's poignant eulogy. The eulogy was delivered by Willie on crutches following a recent safari accident in South Africa. Willie and I were colleagues of about the same seniority in HSBC. Having not served together, we never had the opportunity of getting to know each other well. Willie became a worthy successor to Mike Sandberg in the role of HSBC Group Chairman, and was honoured by a well deserved knighthood for services to banking.

Not long afterwards, Pat died tragically, after a fall in a friend's house in Egerton Crescent.

Whilst living in Egerton Gardens, I was delighted to find I had two old friends as neighbours. One was Bobby Buchanan Michelson, and the other was Lady Wendy Turner. I subsequently enjoyed staying with Bobby and Maxine in their beautifully decorated holiday apartment in Puerto Andratx Majorca. Bobby and his first wife Janie stayed with us in Melbourne in 1968. Bobby had driven out on the London/Sydney car rally, with Janie following by air. He was also a keen power boat racing enthusiast, and had a mercurial career in the London property market, I was much saddened when he died of cancer.

Lady Wendy Turner was the widow of Sir Michael Turner who was the Chief Manager of HSBC, having taken over from Sir Arthur Morse, when I joined the Bank. One day she asked if I would drive her out to Bourne End, where her husband was buried. We managed to find the grave, and I was happy to help her tidy it. Afterwards, we had lunch at a nearby pub and reminisced about Hong Kong in the early 1950's. As the wife of the taipan Wendy hosted the first Tenants Ball at the Chief Manager's house on The Peak. All the expatriate bank staff were asked to come in fancy dress. The occasion was such a success that it became an annual event. It was said that on one occasion a Deputy Chairman, known for his witty sarcasm, was entering the ball accompanied by the Staff Controller. He is said to have remarked to The Staff Controller, "Do you know anybody here?" Whilst serving in Calcutta as accountant he made a comment on the charges return to Head Office, about a family's large medical bills. He said "This family appear to enjoy ill health."

I much admired Wendy for her untiring charity work for the deprived in Hong Kong, and for her interest in the welfare of HSBC foreign and local staff.

Wendy died sometime after I left Egerton Gardens.

Staying with us in Melbourne at the same time as Bobby and Janie was Frank Plugge's younger brother.

Greville. He was doing a sort of two year working walkabout of Australia with some friends. All of us were invited to a birthday party for Dale the daughter of Barrie Harper, a business acquaintance of mine in Melbourne. One of two daughters became a good friend of Prince Charles, and was known as Kanga. In later years she married Lord Tryon and created a well known ladies dress designer label in London before her untimely death.

Tragically, Grevill died in an accident in Morocco.

CHAPTER TWENTY ONE

Odds and Ends

Surfer. On the beach Australia.

Hustler. Mamounia Hotel
Marrakesh billiard room.

Bibliophile.

Gambler. On board Marina
off St. Petersburg.

Lesley and Alexander. Laughing with Mummy.

Golf Marrakesh. Beware of
Cobras in the rough.

Winner American Chamber of.
Commerce Sydney speech contest.

Father. With Alexandra and Skye.

Grandfather. At home with grand daughter Gala.

Dragon Fly painting by Pro Hart.   Scottish West Coast home.

Billiards.

In "The Mikado" lyrics W S Gilbert describes a punishment for billiard cheats along the following line:

"The billiard sharp who anyone catches
His doom is extremely harsh
He will be forced to play extravagant matches
on a cloth untrue
With a twisted cue
with elliptical billiard balls!"

ART

Flying from Sydney to ski in Aspen, I would sometimes stop off at Tahiti. In Tahiti I paid homage to the post impressionist Paul Gauguin at his poignant memorial on the island. By contrast, as a huge admirer of man's artistic achievements, I feel immensely privileged to have seen most of the world's great museums and art galleries.

On a more mundane level, I bought a Pro Hart abstract study of a dragonfly in Sydney in about 1970. After our move to Singapore, I was dismayed to see the pigmentation of the painting disappearing because of ambient climate humidity. With some alarm, I contacted Pro Hart, who was good enough to repaint the work and send it back free of charge. The event, if nothing else, at least makes the provenance more interesting.

Collector

I also have another unusually large rather sombre work by Pro Hart. It is a study of a rotting tree stump called "Termites". Interestingly, Pro Hart used some real termites he embedded in the varnish.

Timothy Klingender, my son in law, was, for a time, a director of Sothebys in Australia, and did much to promote the appreciation of good Australian Aboriginal art.

Through Timothy I was able to learn something about Aboriginal art. However, I never bought into the genre, I find my true passion lies with the out of reach works of portrait artists, such as Gainsborgh and Klimpt, Viewing Klimpt's art in Vienna is very much on my bucket list.

Zinnia persuaded me to commission a lady artist friend of hers to paint a botanical still life of potted orchids. As the painting sits well on Eugenie's Drawing room wall in Rye. I have lent it to her pro temp for her enjoyment.

I have two notable oriental pictures. One is a 1966 signed limited 16/75 Mahayama print I inherited from my darling Lesley. The other is a life size portrait of an important Chinese mandarin woven in fine silk. It will be interesting to look into the origins of his work. I bought it reasonably at a Sydney general auction in 1982.

At the launching of the Embiricos family tanker in Japan, Nick and Valda were presented with a handsome silver model of a galleon by Mitsui the ship builders. As part of the launching party, Mitsui were kind enough to also present Lesley and I with a most attractive framed etched lacquer study of a vase. Martin Sharp, my artist neighbour in Sydney, gave me a limited print of his work "Eternity".

I must admit to being modest about my collection, given that there is much to be modest about! For traditionalists W S Gilbert's mention of art in the operetta "Patience" is worth quoting:

"Be eloquent in praise of the very dull old days which have long since passed away, and convince 'em, if you can, that the reign of good Queen Anne was cultures palmist day.

Of course you will pooh-pooh whatever's fresh and new, and declare it's crude and mean, for art stopped short in the cultivated court of the Empress Josephine."

Japanese print.

Antique woven silk portrait of Chinese court official.

Study of vase etched on lacquer. Ship launching gift to Lesley and I from Mitsui & Co. Japan 1975.

Horse Racing

I was introduced to horse racing by my mother who took me to Ayr races when I was still a schoolboy. She enjoyed the social aspect whilst I was more interested in the cars. I was more impressed with Lord Lonsdale's yellow and black Rolls Royce rather than the horses.

I enjoyed racing in Hong Kong hugely. In 1956 Sir Michael Turner was The HongKong and Shanghai Banking Corporation, Chief Manager, and concurrently Chairman of the Hong Kong Jockey Club. As such he and his wife Wendy would occasionally invite some of the Bank's foreign staff juniors to his box at Happy Valley. There we would have a first class luncheon and a great days racing. Servants would place our bets and, hopefully, return with winnings and the prospect of a tip. Happy Valley was augmented in due course by Sha Tin race course. For some reason I never went there. Racing in Hong Kong benefitted greatly from some of the Russian trainers, one of who's daughters, Lindi, married my friend Willem Mulock Hower.

The bank's lawyers in Singapore were kind enough to invite my wife and I to meetings at Bukit Timah from time to time. It was a good opportunity to meet many of our fellow expatriates.

My great friends Nick and Valda Embiricos were well known racing enthusiasts. One weekend Lesley and I were invited to join their house party at Barkfold Manor. On the Sunday morning all of us went over to Josh Gifford's training stable so that Nick and Valda could discuss running Nick's horse Aldaniti in the Aintree Grand National.

Given that Aldaniti had broken down, and his jockey Bob Champion had been diagnosed with cancer, the chances of the combination winning seemed to be remote to say the least. Whilst stroking Aldaniti Lesley offered him a polo mint. She proffered her hand with the polo mint on it, as well as the remaining mints in silver paper wrapping.

Quick as a flash Aldaniti grabbed the mint AND the mints in the foil wrapping and swallowed the lot. I am pleased to say there were no ill effects. It was decided to enter the horse in the Grand National at Aintree, a formidable course over four miles of two gruelling laps of 16 testing fences the first 14 of which are jumped twice. Before leaving for Australia the next day I asked Nick to place a £10 bet on Aldaniti to win at 66 to 1.

Later in Sydney I switched on the television and was delighted to see the Grand National televised with Aldaniti winning! I telephoned Nick and Valda to offer my congratulations on their horse winning one of the most prestigious races in the world. Josh Gifford was not only a first class horse trainer but was also a good golf player. I played a threesome with him and Johnny Kidd at Sandy Lane in Barbados. What I thought was remarkable about the game was the number of caddies. We had six. One drove the outsize buggy complete with bar, another three carried our respective clubs, another was the fore caddy who went ahead to spot any balls in the rough. Finally there was the caddy who acted as barman. Definitely my idea of relaxed golf! On the subject of golf, I was practising with my son in law Timothy Klingender on the driving range of the Mamounia hotel in Marrakech when we were told about a sign on the nearby Palmeraie course, warning. "Beware of cobras in the rough!"

Valda, a member of the Jockey Club, also served as a jockey club steward for many years, and helped Nick to raise millions for cancer research through the Bob Champion Cancer Trust charity. I have always thought they were never given the recognition they deserved for these services over many years.

On a long hot holiday weekend in Calcutta a bank colleague, Billy Young, and I decided to visit Shillong the capital of Assam. During the flight the hostess distributed broken biscuits, and had to contend with a passenger trying to light a cooking stove at the back of the 'plane. We were the only guests at an old colonial rest house. It was a virtual time warp. Nothing seemed to have changed since before the war. There was rattan chairs covered in faded chintz on the veranda and piles of old Tatler magazines. Even the dead flies on the window sills appeared to be mummified.

The highlight of the visit was the local racing. The ponies were tiny allowing the feet of some of the jockeys to trail on the ground. We enjoyed watching about four races and lost out to the local bookies. At that time India and China had some trouble at the border. There was an Indian army hospital on the outskirts of Shillong over which it was disconcerting to see vultures circling.

HSBC had an annual race day at Sandown Park. In 1997 I attended and much enjoyed catching up with ex HSBC Group Chairman Mike Sandberg. Also there were Peter Hutson and many other old friends.

Over the years I enjoyed Goodwood Races.

Nick and Valda Embiricos almost always had a house party staying for Goodwood week. En route to the course we would stop for a picnic expertly organised by Valda. It was always a pleasure to see Eric and Betty Cooper Keys enjoying Goodwood. Fortified with champagne Eric would take great pleasure in telling his latest jokes. These were gleaned from his habitual perch at the bar of the Army and Navy club. Eric would enthusiastically tell them to anyone who would listen. I did, and enjoyed them hugely.

I had three visits to Royal Ascot. The first two we enjoyed picnics out of the boot of my RR silver spirit. On my last visit with Zinnia we enjoyed the rarefied hospitality of Whites tent. My old friend Hubert Martineau, who raced his horses at Longchamp, was a long time member of Whites and liked to tell amusing stories about the club. He recalled that at one time staff were asked to challenge anyone using the club who they did not recognise. One person was asked if he was a member. The reply was "Oh no, I'm a guest of a non member!" The other story was about a Duke and a member leaving the club after a good lunch and walking down St James's Street. The Duke tipped his hat at a pretty girl. On being asked who the girl was his grace replied "Oh that's me tailor's daughter. The only thing he ever made that fitted me!"

In the early 70's Martin and Aline Parsons invited Lesley and I to stay at Womersley for the St Leger racing festival. If Martin's father was staying he expected everyone to assemble in the drawing room for pre dinner cocktails mixed by himself.

Lord Rosse told me he was taught how to mix drinks in Sloppy Joes in Havana in the 1920's. We enjoyed the racing except for a mishap to Charles Clore's horse. The horse reared in the starting gate and badly injured it's head.

Wendy McWatters was in public relations and was a great friend of Zinnia and Eugenie. She invited Zinnia and I to a reception she was organising for Sheikh Maktoum.

The reception was for the racing fraternity in general and was held in a very large marquee in Newmarket. I was impressed by dozens of servants bearing gold coffee pots, however, I decided to stick to the champagne. I can't recall meeting the Sheikh, even if he was actually there!

In 1969 I attended the Melbourne Cup. A very lively meeting at which I was lucky enough to back the cup winner despite an Aussie punter telling me not to back it. He said he thought the horse was "as devious as a shit house rat!"

On one occasion with Nick and Valda I attended Cheltenham Races. We were box less as Valda's box was not yet completed.

I was standing near Sam Vestey in the paddock when he called out to Nick Embiricos "Come up to the box for a drink". Nick called back

"Which box are you in?" Lord Vestey replied "It's easy to find, it's got E11R on it!".

In the mid 1950's a quartette of us being myself, Brian Critchley, Gawaine Baillie, and Michael Shurey took an interest in greyhound racing at White City. It was always left to Brian to make the bookings as it was his father, General Critchley, who was a founding member of White City greyhound racing.

We would invite girlfriends and all of us would enjoy dinner behind glass over the finishing post. Thanks to Brian's father's connection we were treated like VIPs and somehow it all seemed so much more convenient than the conventional daytime sport of kings. General Critchley and his wife were both championship golfers. They had an impressive house on Wentworth Estate. I visited them once with Brian. The whole house was festooned with tape so that the General, who had sadly become blind, could navigate his way around. Tragically Brian Critchley died shortly after in the West Indies.

Footnote

Alas, Nick forgot to place my bet. He did, however, buy me a good dinner to help make up for my loss!

Politics

Bob Hawke the Australian Prime Minister was a Rhodes scholar at Oxford. He was reputed to have a mind like a steel trap. He entered politics through his work with the Australian Trade Unions.

On the brighter side of Australian politics was a remark attributed to a Prime Minister at a UN conference. The conference was about the allocation of refugees to various countries. At one stage, it is said, the Australian Prime Minister suddenly exclaimed "Christ, don't give us the Shiites!" On another occasion whilst on the hustings in Perth, it is said

Bob Hawk was caught on camera with an old woman who had thrust her face in his saying "what about the pensioners ya mongrel!"

There are so many stories about Churchill. One of my favourites is, on being told Clement Attlee, his arch socialist rival, was a modest man, Churchill, replied "Yes, he has much to be modest about!"

I also liked the story about the Australian dream. "A million Kiwis swimming back to New Zealand with a Pom under each arm.

SKIING

Partly because of a combination of lack of nerve and opportunity, I never became really good at skiing. To be fair to myself I did manage some of the Mt. Ajax mogul free blue runs at Aspen. My skiing holidays were never more than a week and because of weather it was rare to have a whole week of uninterrupted skiing.

One of my most memorable skiing holidays was over a long weekend in Japan. Japan was still occupied during the winter of 1959.

Mimi MacArthur the American Ambassadors's daughter invited a party of us to the American skiing reservation at Shiga Heights.

A private train was provided and an entire skiing area was cordoned off exclusively for us. We also had the exclusive use of a Japanese inn situated at the bottom of the ski run. There was nothing better than to finish ones ski run and hop in to the hot spring spa within the inn. That would be followed by a massage, sukiyaki and lots of sake. Afterwards we slept soundly in our yukatas on the futons laid out on the tatami floor.

On one occasion I actually received a minor prize for competing in an amateur down hill slalom at Shrocken a ski jumping village in Austria. The prize was a small bronze badge shaped like a single ski. How I managed to complete the run let alone finish 3rd I'll never know.

As a family we enjoyed skiing at Val d'Isere. We rented a self catering apartment in the village and really enjoyed the local boulangerie and charcuterie.

Most winters there was enough snow to ski at either Falls Creek or Thredbo in Australia. At Thredbo we witnessed the landing on the moon on television in the company of stockbroker Charles Goode who was later to become Chairman of ANZ bank. On the same day I put out my shoulder on a sledge mishap. My accountant Bill Charlton frequently invited the family to ski at his shared chalet in Falls Creek. In the early 1970's the facilities were pretty basic but we were all grateful for any skiing at all. Bib Stillwell and his wife Gillian were frequent guests at the Falls Creek chalet. Bib owned one of the biggest Ford agencies in Australia. He also had the Learjet agency for Australia.

Following a remarkable sales run of Learjets in his territory he was elected President of Learjet to be based in Tucson Arizona. At that time Learjet was partially owned by the Gates Corporation and one of Bib's perquisites was the use of the companies' large luxurious ski chalet in Aspen.

If we were going to London from Australia we would, at Bib's invitation, plan a few days skiing at Aspen.

Leaving Aspen for Denver by Learjet.

Usually we would spend a few days en route at either Hawaii or Tahiti then on to Los Angeles and thence to Denver. After staying the night in Denver I would be up early to rent a car for the drive up to Aspen. It was depressing to see queues of men seeking work at 6am in the freezing cold of Denver. At other times Bib would pick us up at Denver airport usually in a brand new Learjet. By law the Learjet had to have two pilots. Bib's co pilot was always an attractive blonde girl. Although she desperately wanted to clock up flying hours Bib always insisted in piloting the 'plane himself.

He would tirelessly joke "Confucius he say, lady pilot who fly upside down have crack up".

My job was to pour the vintage Krug on the flight. The very long gentle ski run at Buttermilk was a godsend for our daughters Alexandra and Skye. Vail was less than an hours drive away and we also enjoyed some skiing there.

My worst skiing experience was in Flaine France. Bill Charlton and I arrived in bad weather which continued for three days. On the fourth day a group of us hired a guide to take us up the mountain above the bad weather. All went well until the descent. I was trailing the group, had a fall and was left behind. Darkness fell, and I became disoriented and hopelessly lost. Somehow or other I managed to find my way down the mountain in the dark guided by the braying sounds, smell, and bells of the sledge donkeys in the village.

In 1990 I visited my cousin Ian McCardle and his wife in Cyprus. We were persuaded to go to the Aphrodite grotto where Lesley could not wait to strip off and jump into the Aphrodite pool. It is said that if you immerse yourself in the pool you will not age and have eternal beauty. What woman could resist that? Sadly my darling Lesley died of a brain tumour within a year, so in a fateful way her wish not to age came true.

After visiting the Aphrodite grotto we went up to Troodos on Mt Olympus to the ski resort. Alas, there was no snow.

At one time I owned an apartment in Montreux Switzerland. The nearest skiing run was on Rochers de Naye a mountain overlooking the town easily accessible by the amazing cogwheel train. Gstaad was about 2 hours away by car or train. I never skied Gstaad as both my visits there were off season. I did however enjoy the spectacle of blonde coloured cattle being herded through the picturesque town with their Alpine bells jangling.

On a visit to Vancouver I took the opportunity of driving up to Mt Whistler. I enjoyed some skiing there and the opportunity of seeing black bears in the wild. We were told the best way to see the bears was to go to the local rubbish tip. We did this and were rewarded with close ups of the Bears.

The future of banking

Conceivably, well into the future,banks as we know them, will disappear. Instead, a single universal credit authority might be created. Notes and coins, cheques, currency exchange rates, etc., could all become curiosities of the past. An innovative measure of value the UC (Universal Credit) might well become the only global settlement currency, controlled by a fail proof world credit authority. Personal accounts could conceivably be operated by means of smart sophisticated wearable biomimetic digital secure devices, light years more advanced than those already appearing. In such a future world, credit providers might well be able to offer browser access to a range of holograms programmed to promote new products, answer FAQs, and even conduct preliminary loan application interviews. If we can be certain of anything, I feel sure gold will always remain a sought after store of value. This Orwellian snapshot scenario into a super digital/robotic future might seem, to some, too far fetched, perhaps beyond fiction?

Sotogrande

My best man, Billy Hargroves, could't wait to retire early at the end of his career with HSBC. I think he became weary of the bank's culture and of living in the Far East. After retirement he and his wife Elizabeth lived in Ireland for a spell before moving to Sotogrande. They were kind enough to invite me to stay from time to time. Amongst the retired expatriates living in Sotogrande were Peter Barnard, who I knew from his time with Swires in Hong Kong, and Jerry Tait who was a contemporary of mine with HSBC.

Jerry lived with his new wife and baby in nearby Marbella in a splendid hacienda type house in the centre of town. In his house Jerry would serve some of the best bloody Mary's ever, even surpassing those of the Captains Bar in The Mandarin Hotel, Hong Kong.

Billy had formed a friendship with Jeremy Lowndes who I had met years earlier in Sydney. Both Jeremy Lowndes and Billy enjoyed having refreshments. Rumours were strongly denied that the pair kept Johnny Walker in overtime!

Jeremy Lowndes was to go to prison for several years in Spain over the tragic death of his wife. According to one source. It seems that one night they were having an alcohol fuelled argument at the dining table. For some reason Jeremy took a swipe at his wife with a candle holder. Unfortunately the blow connected and tragically his wife died.

Lord Keith and his wife also enjoyed living part of the year in Sotogrande.

I had met them in London several times before at dinner parties given by my companion Zinnia Judd. Kenneth Keith was an amusing raconteur and I particularly enjoyed his anecdotes about the cut and thrust days when he was running Hill Samuel the Merchant bank. Kenneth Keith also had a hand in establishing Macquarie Bank in Australia.

Flying in to Gibraltar was almost as daunting as flying in to Kai Tak airport. I'm not sure what was worse, flying over Chinese laundry poles or towards the Gibraltar cliff face dead ahead.

San Rocco was the railway station for Gibraltar and it was from there that I took the express train for a round trip to Madrid. I had visited Madrid before but had no time to properly enjoy the Prado. The outward train journey was comfortable and enjoyable. Alas, the train broke down on the return journey and we were all decanted into buses for the long trip back to San Rocco. Nevertheless, although low on my bucket list, my second visit to the Prado was well worth the discomfort endured on the return journey.

I enjoyed many duty free shopping visits to Gibraltar, and once managed a day trip visit to Tangier.

Whilst in Gibraltar I was surprised to learn that David Lochhead, my army friend in Scotland, had gone on to serve in Gibraltar. He had met and married one of the Governor's daughters. He became General Secretary of the Red Cross (Scotland) for many years after his army career.

Nightmare on the Peak

Whilst awaiting our move to Mackinnon House in Mount Austin Road, with it's enviable tennis court and canons on the lawn, we took over Dr Vio's more modest house on the Peak. Dr Vio was a leading physician in the colony, and had gone on leave prior to retirement.

On our first night in the Dr's house, we were awakened by the terrifying sound of heavy breathing accompanied by what sounded like a heavy chain being dragged in the basement below our ground floor bedroom. Uncaring about loss of face, I must admit I was too scared to go down in to the cellar to investigate. With visions of Frankenstein monsters, I simply locked our bedroom door, and cringed under the bed linen.

The next morning, accompanied by the No.1 boy (Butler), I opened the cellar door. To my horror, I discovered a man sized ape like creature with staring eyes, covered in brown and purple hair, in chains! Had I discovered the creature the night before, I feel sure I would have died of fright.

It turned out that it was a fully grown orang utan being treated by Dr Vio with gentian violet ointment for a skin condition. That morning the Chinese owner arrived to collect his pet. I was told later that the anthropoid's skin condition had cleared up, and it was living a comfortable life with it's owner.

I shall never forget the nightmare experience of hearing it's heavy breathing and chain rattling in the middle of a dark foggy sleepless night on the Peak.

CHAPTER TWENTY TWO

India

My experiences in India pale into insignificance when compared to those of my daughter's Alexandra and Skye. They both had some hair raising adventures back backing through India, Nepal, Tibet. and Ladakh. Amongst other things, they had to endure +50 degrees heatwave amidst power cuts in Rajasthan,and nail biting sheer cliff drop mountain pass bus trips in Ladakh.

All very interesting, but that is their story, not mine.

CHAPTER TWENTY THREE

Conclusion

Taking time to review my life has given me the opportunity to reflect on what has influenced me most. After family, friends, and elders, I'm afraid self advancement must be high on the list, but close to that,I have often felt a subconscious awareness of the ever present pressures of the world's miseries. The horror of poverty, never ending war from the carnage of WW1 followed by WW2 and beyond,amply bears out Robert Burn's words about "Man's inhumanity to man." Dare I mention the spectre of financial Armageddon! It seems so easy to be pessimistic about the state of humanity, yet there are millions of good deeds done and many friendships forged every day, of which we know nothing. Shakespeare told us about the evil that men do living after them, the good being often interred with their bones.

Weather is a subject most of us know something about. Having had much tropical sunshine in my life, I am grateful to be living on the West Coast of Scotland. They say if my view of the islands is blurred, it's raining, and if I can see clearly it's going to rain. Nowadays, ocean views, sea air, and lots of rain, and some sunshine, are the ingredients of my idea of the perfect climate.

In music terms, the climate of SW Scotland could aptly be described as a fusion of Vivaldi's The Four Seasons and the more dramatic elements of Mendelssohn's Scottish symphony score. Perhaps with a bit of McCartney's Mull of Kintyre thrown in.

Being born in Scotland, I suppose I could be likened to an old salmon who has found it's way home.

Lightning Source UK Ltd.
Milton Keynes UK
UKOW03f2359140217
294432UK00001B/114/P